Beyond Winning

SMART PARENTING IN A TOXIC SPORTS ENVIRONMENT

Kim John Payne,
Luis Fernando Llosa, and
Scott Lancaster

LYONS PRESS
Guilford, Connecticut

An imprint of Globe Pequot Press

Lyons Press is an imprint of Globe Pequot Press.

All illustrations courtesy of Katharine Payne

Project editor: Ellen Urban
Layout: Mary Ballachino

Library of Congress Cataloging-in-Publication Data is available on
file.

ISBN 978-0-7627-8665-7

Printed in the United States of America

10 9 8 7 6 5 4 3 2 1

In some cases identifying details, including names, have been changed
to preserve the anonymity of parents or children.

To all parents who remember the joy of unhurried, creative play and wish to give this most precious of all gifts to their own children. Many blessings on your parenting path.

KJP

For Mary, my guiding light, and for our fabulous five: Chai, Isabel, Will, Gabriel, and Inigo, who have taught me everything I know and don't know about parenting and coaching.

LFLL

For my son Justin, who has taught me the most important reasons behind participation and sports. To Xiomara for her inspiration, support, and all that I continue to learn from her.

SL

If we apply the wisdom we find in *Beyond Winning,* we have a better shot at making youth sports a more positive experience. So, get involved! I did, just as my son and daughter were starting to play soccer nine years ago. I didn't have any big plans back then to change the face of New York City soccer, but one thing sort of leads to another . . . as you will find out. In the end, nothing is more important than the lessons ALL our children can learn from playing on a team where they are encouraged to take risks, learn from their mistakes, accept differences, and persevere. Such experiences serve them their whole lives.

—Dana DiPrima, Commissioner, West Side Soccer League, NYC; the largest all-volunteer, AYSO region in the United States (4,000 players ages 5 to 18 and 6,000-plus parents, who support more than 400 recreational, tournament, and competitive travel teams)

Contents

INTRODUCTION **vii**

NAVIGATING THIS BOOK **xvi**

CHAPTER 1: Parenting a Whole Child through Sports **1**

CHAPTER 2: Your Sports Biography—Does It Hinder or Help? **16**

CHAPTER 3: Too Much, Too Soon **43**

CHAPTER 4: The Power of Play **71**

CHAPTER 5: How to Avoid Creating Entitlement Monsters—Bullying, Trash Talk, Elitism, and Other Assorted Sports Ills **100**

CHAPTER 6: You Are Your Child's First Coach—Freeing Your Child from Oppressive, Hyperorganized Sports **126**

CHAPTER 7: And in All Things . . . Balance and Flow **149**

CHAPTER 8: Beyond Winning—A New Paradigm for Youth Sports Competition **189**

ACKNOWLEDGMENTS **215**

BIBLIOGRAPHY **216**

INDEX **218**

ABOUT THE AUTHORS **222**

Introduction

Every child's life unfolds in its own unique way. Our role as parents is to nurture our children and guide them as they grow into strong, healthy, independent individuals. How then can we shield our children from today's intoxicating youth sports culture, which sweeps us all into its swirling vortex and subjects our kids to too much, too soon? Caught up in a cultural frenzy, we clutter our children's daily lives with too many sporting activities and, though often unwittingly, pressure our "child-athletes" to perform. As a result they grow up too quickly, and often the foundations of our family lives are fractured.

At Whole Child Sports we want to slow things down a bit and give kids the time they need to develop wholesomely. They will thrive and can reach their full potential as athletes and adults if they are taught in developmentally appropriate stages. Ours is a holistic approach to teaching sports to children. To begin with, we, as parents, can train ourselves to change the way we think as a first step toward providing a healthier sports experience for them. If we can abandon our fantasies of vicarious stardom, if we can take a few steps back and give our kids some space to grow and learn, and if we can temper our expectations and become more mindful, the fog will lift. Then, with clarity, we can create a fun-filled, relatively pressure-free environment in which our children can flourish.

In this book we offer an alternative approach to teaching sports to kids that de-emphasizes short-term goals like winning games and youth championships and discourages the early introduction of adult-oriented, league-structured competition. We recommend that parents learn more about their own sports biographies so that they can temper their influence over their child's sports experiences, which, in the younger years, should include a healthy diet of free play and loosely structured skill-building activities. This approach includes training techniques and coaching strategies aimed at developing core strength, balance, and creativity in aspiring athletes, and it educates parents and coaches alike about our four stages of age-appropriate, healthy play.

What is abundantly clear is that we, as parents, need to take action. That's why Scott Lancaster, Kim John Payne, and I have formed Whole Child Sports. We come from disparate professional and personal backgrounds but are united in our growing alarm at the toxic nature of today's youth sports culture. Increased television coverage, big money sponsorship, and the predominance of a win-at-all-costs mentality, promoted by misguided coaches and overbearing parents, have all contributed to the poisoning of childhood sports experiences, which should be fun, skill building, and stress-free.

Let's take a closer look at today's toxic youth sports mindset. Why do even the most conscientious parents and educators devolve into did-you-win drones when talking to kids about their experiences on the field? Instead of "Was it fun?" it's always, "Did you win?" "What was the score?" "Well, at least it was close, right?" We've all engaged in this conversation or overheard it countless times. And the message to our kids is crystal clear: Winning is the ultimate goal, the answer to everything, the holy grail of athletic pursuit.

When such cultural attitudes are pervasive, sportsmanship, fair play, and, most important, learning—which should be paramount for kids playing sports up to the age of eighteen—are sacrificed at the altar of victory. Parents focus on winning. They make financial and family-time decisions in service to victory. Coaches make team decisions, from participation to player playing time to training priorities, in deference to winning.

As ESPN's Tom Farrey points out in *Game On: How the Pressure to Win at All Costs Endangers Youth Sports and What Parents Can Do About It,* his eye-opening account of the youth sports landscape, the obsession with early success in a win-at-all-costs culture has created a pressure chamber in which top prospects, even at the age of five or six, are funneled into elite programs while the majority of kids—the "weak ones"—are robbed of the opportunity to discover and develop their talents.

Where's the fun and athletic development? And what about the steep human cost? In this ultracompetitive culture, the darkest demons of the sports world run rampant. Cheating, physical and emotional abuse, bullying, and violence become endemic. The result is a youth sports landscape pockmarked with children who end up—at age eleven or twelve—with fractured egos, low self-esteem, and, in some cases, severe physical injuries. It's why millions of American kids quit organized sports just as they become teenagers. And why thousands of parents we've spoken to are so anxious and concerned.

The tens of thousands of volunteers who dedicate much, if not all, of their weekends (and many weeknights) to organize, coach, and support youth sports programs do so with the best of intentions. We all want what's best for our children. But what many of us parents and coaches are unaware of is that there are more dynamic and holistic ways for our children to learn, play, and compete than that old-school approach we were exposed to as kids.

Epictetus once said, "It is impossible for a man to learn what he thinks he already knows." These insightful words help explain why youth sports has evolved so little or—to be candid—devolved so much in the United States over the past twenty-five years. Think about it. What has changed since we were kids? We grew up participating in a system that mimics professional and elite-level sports. It's a setup defined by scheduled practices, league play, and, at its pinnacle, elite travel team competition. The people who run organized sports—let's call them traditionalists—promote the status quo. It's what they know, are comfortable with, and can control.

Late Hall of Fame NFL football coach Bill Walsh argued, "A good coach never stops learning and always keeps an open mind." As parents and coaches we should all take heed. It's time we think about changing the traditional framework of youth sports. We know change doesn't come easily, especially when it threatens a long-standing culture that has established and validated the identities of thousands of individuals—coaches, league administrators, commissioners—within their communities. But our youth sports system is deeply flawed. The kids have made it clear: More than 70 percent quit organized sports by the age of thirteen. It's time to redefine the paradigm.

Our own personal youth sports stories follow, which we've included to give you a clear sense of each of our backgrounds and our collective experience in this field.

Luis Fernando Llosa

As a former investigative reporter at *Sports Illustrated* and a father of five, I have observed the full gamut of sports experiences at all levels, from elite to peewee. While reporting on age fraud and steroid abuse, I was exposed to the dark underbelly of sports. I wrote about pro athletes who pumped themselves with toxic fluids to play better, train harder, and secure bigger multimillion-dollar contracts, and impressionable children who—driven by pushy parents—imitated their athletic idols, taking performance-enhancing drugs themselves.

One parent I reported on falsified his son's age so that the teenager could dazzle millions with his pitching prowess in the 2001 Little League World Series. Another forced his child to take human growth hormone and testosterone, starting at the age of thirteen, in order to transform him into a world-class inline skater. The first dad was disgraced, the second imprisoned. But what pains and motivates me most is a much more common occurrence. It's what I see again and again when I coach my kids or just goof around with them on a golf course: parents who publicly berate their kids. They put them down for not scoring a goal or not making an aggressive enough tackle. One evening I came upon a child on a putting green, just shy of two years old. As I looked on, his father, unprompted, informed me that his son was a terrible putter, that he couldn't play at all. What I saw was an innocent child who could barely grasp a club, let alone line up a putt. What I foresaw was a life of pressure, guilt, and disappointment, and the stifling of unlimited potential.

It's disturbing to think what outsize expectations can do to hope. Another time, a child came up to me on the first day of team practice and asked excitedly if she could be our goalie. Before I could respond, her father blurted out, "Don't let her play in goal. She has terrible hands." The ten-year-old looked shell-shocked and turned beet red. I put her in goal that very day. Admittedly, she was shaky between the pipes, but by the end of the season she had developed into a confident keeper.

Scott Lancaster

What troubles me most about today's youth sports culture is that children are not the primary focus. The fields and courts are overrun by self-absorbed coaches who live out fantasies of power and control at the expense of the kids they "coach." The "adults" get too caught up in the hype of winning games and championships, when they should concentrate solely on training kids to master the fundamentals of the sports they play. Every one of the hundreds of NCAA Division I college football and basketball coaches I've interviewed decries the stark decline in skill development in youth sports. The players they coach at the elite college level too often arrive on campus unable to properly execute fundamental skills such as tackling, blocking, rebounding, or pivoting. College coaches are forced to painstakingly "reteach" the fundamentals.

It would help if children in youth sports programs were not treated like adults. They are taught adult versions of sports, with rules created for adults on full-size fields. Skill development should be the aim, not competition. When I worked as director of youth development at the National Football League (NFL), we launched the Junior Player Development (JPD) program. We broke practices down into ten-minute rotating instructional drill segments that taught specific fundamental skills. We played flag football and seven-on-seven games instead of full-squad scrimmages, because they are much more effective in developing and honing game-sequence skills. Most important, we tailored practices and drills to specific age groups. The kids loved the intensity and diversity of the drill stations and developed into well-rounded athletes. They did not complain about wanting to play on teams in "leagues." Several JPD program initiates eventually made it to the NFL.

But shortsighted parents fretted that what their kids were learning was not "real football." They clamored for helmets, pads, tackling, and full-squad games. Since their kids weren't replicating what they saw the pros do on television, they figured they were not learning *the right stuff.* Can we change our attitudes and expectations as parents? Can we focus on finding the best ways to help our children learn? The endgame of youth sports is not to entertain adults, but to develop children's athletic skills while fanning their budding passion for the sports they are learning to play.

Change does not come easily. When I coached my nine-year-old son's local football team, I sought to make minor rule changes to minimize the risk of injuries during kickoffs, punts, and returns. Yet a group of coaches adamantly opposed the modifications. They couldn't bear to see "the game" adulterated. When I insisted, I was stonewalled and, ultimately, drummed out of the league. Together, we, the parents, can revolutionize youth sports. That's what the Whole Child Sports approach is about. Our aim is not to fill trophy cases but to work on the long-term development of young athletes. Parent by parent, coach by coach, we can work to change this misguided sports culture from the inside out.

Kim John Payne

The shift in parents questioning the too much, too soon, too hard, too young culture has been remarkable. I have been a kind of parenting troubadour, traveling the world giving countless lectures, classes, and workshops on this theme, and I have seen the question of pushing kids too early move from the fringes right into the center of what parents are thinking about.

Something is wrong, very wrong, with what we are being told is "normal" for our kids, and a large number of parents are looking for a way to articulate what is for most a gut instinct. Parents are also looking for a sensible alternative that does not force them to turn their lifestyles upside down, a shift that can flow into their families but nevertheless set a new and much healthier trajectory for their children. After making a change in his family life away from the sensory overwhelm that has become the new normal toward a more considered approach, one parent said recently, "I feel like I am standing on my own ground now. Before, I was feeling pushed around by a bunch of expectations. Everything has gotten easier." On the other hand, the parents of an elite downhill skiing daughter told me after a workshop that "the whole thing is tearing our family apart. It's completely out of control, and we need to do something about it."

When I worked as a volunteer with children in war zones and refugee camps, I came to recognize the look of overwhelm and trauma. I see this same look in the eyes of so many children in North America. While our children are not experiencing the physical privations that come from living in a war zone, of course, they are, nonetheless, in the midst of an undeclared war on childhood, and heading up the list of the potential aggressors is a sporting experience that is pushing them way too hard when they are way too young.

I rose through the junior sports ranks in my birth country of Australia to an elite national youth level, both in swimming and soccer. Competitive swimming can be fairly described as a national obsession in Australia. How else does this country with a tiny population regularly rank in the top three Olympic medal winners in the world? I personally experienced glimmers of the best that sport can give, and for that I'm grateful. But I was also exposed to the deep darkness of the worst in the harsh overtraining and manipulation of children. Like many other former elite youth athletes, I now live with significant physical injuries caused by the unrelenting grind of training to be the best.

There is something utterly wonderful about play, games, and sport. I have been a high school basketball coach since the 1980s and have shared in amazing results, both in terms of outcomes on the court and the growth of emotional health and social intelligence that are possible when sport is approached in a way that puts the child's development first.

Parents all around the world are looking for ways to navigate child and youth sports. The time for raising Whole Children through sports has arrived, and its potential is vast.

Navigating This Book

As parents ourselves, we understand that it's virtually impossible to find the time to sit down and read a book from cover to cover, so we've tried to do three things: (1) lay out eight self-contained chapters that explore major sports parenting topics and can be read separately; (2) turn within each chapter to the questions we've heard most often from parents over the years and formulate discussions that examine the various issues and concerns we all have; and (3) then move on to develop practical solutions. That's what makes this book different—the focus on solutions. That's what parents have asked us to provide.

When you look through these chapters, trust your instinct. Go right to where your gut takes you. That's a great place to begin, and perhaps that's where your most urgent sports parenting questions lie. Chances are you will discover something that we really value here at Whole Child Sports: *the small doable change.* Even a tiny change in trajectory, a small initial shift in a direction that feels natural, sets your child's sports life on a new course that will expand as the seasons roll on and she engages in a healthier, more dynamic experience.

CHAPTER 1

Parenting a Whole Child through Sports

We've all had fun playing sports and watching our children play. We know the positives. But we can't ignore the dark side: the pressure, the bullying, the elitism, the lack of playfulness, and the stifling of creativity. Whole Child Sports speaks directly to the many parents who feel that though today's youth sports culture is toxic, it can be transformed into a better learning and living environment for our children. We are all in this together, and to change how our children experience sports, we must work together.

There are dozens of books that decry the toxic atmosphere of youth sports today and offer good general advice to parents. But most of them take a performance-oriented view. While sports psychologists and coaching experts rightly suggest that parents step back and concentrate more on fun, the underlying dynamic always seems to cycle back to performance. They don't zero in on the heart of the problem—that our culture is steeped in a mind-set that imprisons us and our children in incessant judgment. We are very goal oriented, and that's fine, but our aim should not be to develop performance princes and divas, but rather to provide our children with opportunities

1

to become more well-rounded, supple, adaptive, and creative. That is what will serve them best in the broader context of their lives, both now and in the future.

We are living in a world in which the first question we ask our children after any game they play is, "Did you win?" and we're suggesting a somewhat radical shift that can best be summed up by "How did it go?" Because the first question—which is usually followed up by "Did you score?" or "How many points did you make?"—frames their experience too narrowly. It spotlights the short-term outcome. If they have won, they have a positive answer to give you. If they played well and were key contributors, then they've shown you that they are worthy of your affection and approval. But if they lost or didn't contribute much, the conversation—and your connection with them—hits a brick wall.

Why not frame your query more openly, by asking them to share their experiences rather than report performance statistics? In doing that, you redefine both your child's experience in sports and what you value as most important. It opens up a window through which your children can connect with you and discuss the many facets of their encounters on the field or court with teammates and opponents, as well as off it, in the locker room or on the bus.

This might seem like a minor concern, but it is really a central issue and at the heart of the Whole Child Sports approach. When the question is "Did you win?" it's a mismatch. We are disconnecting ourselves from our children's deeper reality. We are closing a door. We risk showing them we just don't get it: We really don't understand what's going on for them, and in them, and why they spend their time and effort participating in the first place. Because, as we'll point out in this book, most kids play sports for fun and friendship. It's personal. They also want to stretch and challenge themselves. They enjoy learning and getting better. It gives them a broader sense of self; it develops their self-esteem and self-definition.

To be clear, we are not antiwinning. What we want is to redefine winning. So let's put the scoreboard in the proper perspective, as one informative yardstick of success. That makes it part of a larger whole, just one among several measures of developmental progress.

With a combined eighty years of coaching experience between us, we are convinced that when you redefine success in this way, you connect with a kid's deepest motivation for playing sports in the first place. There's nothing soft, weak, or "everyone-gets-a-trophy"–ish about Whole Child Sports. By developing the Whole Child—the Whole Athlete—we help young athletes play to the edge of their potential, to reach optimal creative performance. In other words, to enter a state of flow, or what's more commonly known in the sports world as "the zone." That is when they are at their best and, as an indirect benefit, are much more likely to win more often. And they will enter into this mind-set not just in games but also in practice. As they walk out of the gym or off the field to head home, this sense of flow follows and positively affects so much else going on in their lives.

Chapter 2: Your Sports Biography—Does It Hinder or Help?

In this chapter we examine why parents can become so vested in their child's athletic success that they inadvertently sour his sports experiences. We provide parents with psychological techniques they can use to avoid falling into the trap of identifying too closely with their kid's performance. We tend to project our hopes and fears onto our children. When we mine the depth of our own childhood sports biographies, we can come to terms with any positive or unpleasant experiences we may have had. If we learn to be more mindful of our influence over our children and take a few steps back, we can create the space that allows them to experience the joys and challenges of sports in their own unique way.

Here are some of the topics you'll encounter:

- Your sports history influences your child
- Why am I so critical after my child's game?
- The most common underlying reasons parents overreact when their kids play sports
- The most common anger triggers
- Why shouldn't we want to win at all costs?

Chapter 3: Too Much, Too Soon

Today's sports culture exposes children to *too much, too soon*. We want to apply the brakes a bit and give kids time to grow at a more appropriate pace. In this chapter we emphasize free play and loosely structured skill-building activities in the younger years, and we encourage self-discovery as parents learn to mitigate their influence on their children's sports experiences. As they grow older, guided by coaches trained to cultivate the Whole Child—not just the aspiring athlete—they can develop into creative, flexible, healthy young men and women who are confident and well prepared for competitive play on life's many fields.

Here are some of the topics you'll encounter:

- When should my child start organized sports?
- Can competitive sports affect my child's friendships?
- What do I do if my child hates practice?
- Too much pressure too soon
- Faking injuries: a doctor's story

Chapter 4: The Power of Play

Remember when you were a kid and showed up daily at the sandlot or park to play pickup ball with your neighborhood friends? Those days are long gone in most communities. Take a stroll through the fields and parks in your town or city. You'll commonly see toddlers playing freely and happily in and around playgrounds, but most kids five and up are much more likely to be standing in groups listening to an adult jaw about rules, player position, or strategy, or playing their hearts out on a field or court, surrounded by adults screaming "encouragement" or mumbling disappointedly about botched scoring opportunities. Adults have an irresistible urge to organize and control. Children just want to have fun.

We encourage parents to nurture and protect the time and space children need to engage in unstructured free play. It is essential to their physical, emotional, and social growth, and helps them become more adaptive, creative, and dynamic athletes and youngsters as they begin their journey in organized sports at an appropriate age.

Here are some of the topics you'll encounter:

- Are organized sports eroding my child's imagination?
- A team pulls together

- Is there value to free play?
- The double edge of play
- Do boys and girls play differently?

Chapter 5: How to Avoid Creating Entitlement Monsters—Bullying, Trash Talk, Elitism, and Other Assorted Sports Ills

We delve into the subjects of trash talk, bullying, unhealthy competition, team hierarchy, favoritism, and sportsmanship within today's toxic youth sports context and provide suggestions and solutions for creating a healthier setting for your child's athletic development.

Here are some of the topics you'll encounter:

- A coach, a player, and bullying
- What can I do about trash talk?
- Why can't my child be team captain?
- Does it create a sense of entitlement when my kid wears his jersey to school?
- Is it harmful for my child to see so much sports violence on television?

Chapter 6: You Are Your Child's First Coach—Freeing Your Child from Oppressive, Hyperorganized Sports

In this chapter we explore a parent's role in developing and tailoring a child's early sports experiences. Moms and dads are their child's first coaches. We offer suggestions for exercises, activities, and programs that are fun and developmentally appropriate for younger kids. We encourage parents to introduce children ages five to eleven, and older, to games that develop their movement skills, balance, and coordination. These are not outcome-oriented games. The emphasis is on fun and skill development. We strongly recommend home sports schooling for this age group and offer specific examples of backyard games and park activities that can help develop balance and movement skills, and creative thinking. They are fun focused and don't require too much adult involvement and direction.

Toward the end of the chapter we shift gears a bit to focus more on older kids, ages twelve and up. At this stage organized sports come into play. We offer advice on choosing the best coach for your kid and arm you with a list of signs that your child's coach (or a coach you may be considering for your child) may be driven more by ego fulfillment than by a desire to nurture young athletes.

Here are some of the topics you'll encounter:

- What if I have no prior coaching experience?
- How can I foster my child's athletic potential?
- Sports equipment for your home coaching
- Can moms coach, too?
- Choosing a coach: a parent's checklist

Chapter 7: And in All Things . . . Balance and Flow

Starting in chapter 7 we focus more on children ages twelve and up, and in this chapter you will notice a shift in the terminology we use. We substitute the term *child* with the term *youth*. To clarify, we refer to a child under the age of twelve as a *child* and a child twelve and up as a *youth* or *young athlete*. So when you see the term *Whole Youth* rather than *Whole Child,* you'll know we are referring to the older age group. This is a great time for kids to segue into organized sports. We explore various facets of balance in youth sports: how parents and youth athletes can juggle family time and school commitments with youth sports schedules, as well as social and emotional balance in relation to sports. We also provide a basic guideline for learning and developing physical balancing skills, speed, and conditioning, which are the cornerstones of a young athlete's physical athletic foundation.

Here are some of the topics you'll encounter:

- How can I manage the financial cost of youth sports?
- What if my kid is too passive?
- The proper balance between training and playing
- Four ways to develop balance and stability in a young athlete
- Ten tenets of a balanced Whole Youth Sports experience

Chapter 8: Beyond Winning—A New Paradigm for Youth Sports Competition

In this chapter we profile parents in an Ossining, New York, football league who have changed the way sports are taught to their children, and we present a new paradigm for youth sports competition that focuses every training session and game on long-term developmental goals and de-emphasizes game results and scores. We offer parents a Whole Youth Sports training and competition blueprint, which includes key principles like teaching every athlete every position and incorporating small-space training and competitions in every practice; provide a sample alternative scorecard that coaches and parents can use to score a player's performance in a more developmentally focused way; and lay out a sample practice plan, as part of a thematically centered, well-organized guide to training a team holistically throughout a season.

Here are some of the topics you'll encounter:

- A new paradigm for youth sports competition
- A Whole Youth Sports training session blueprint
- Every athlete learns every position
- Measuring games beyond the scoreboard

Finding a Road Map to Change with a Focus on Developmental Stages

Finding a road map to change is a challenging task. Advocates for change have decried the disheartening state of youth sports for decades. In 1981, Fred Engh founded the National Youth Sports Alliance, an organization dedicated to fostering change. In 2002, he wrote *Why Johnny Hates Sports: Why Organized Youth Sports Are Failing Our Children and What We Can Do About It,* a seminal exposé of abuses in youth sports. One year earlier, Bob Bigelow, another champion for change, coauthored *Just Let the Kids Play: How to Stop Other Adults from Ruining Your Child's Fun and Success in Youth Sports.* Both men and many others have worked tirelessly to make a difference.

Yet despite the efforts of grassroots groups like Engh's and the American Youth Sports Organization, which promote fun and fair play while de-emphasizing winning, the sad truth is that the core problems in youth sports persist on a massive scale.

The first step toward revolutionizing youth sports, toward restoring the sanity and simplicity of its two most basic goals—fun and fundamentals—is to chip away at today's cultural mind-set, to develop a shift in attitude. Then we can focus on the nuts and bolts: developing our children's movement and balance skills while fostering their creativity and passion for play.

Whole Child Sports discourages the use of adult-structured games, rules, and regulation-size playing areas in youth sports until high school age, because such adult-centric parameters are detrimental to the proper development of young athletes. That's why we offer a four-stage timeline for the age-appropriate development of a young athlete, based on a child's physical, psychological, and neurological development, rather than her perceived talents or prospects.

Truth be told, no one can know what a child's potential is at an early age. You can't trust a coach who claims that your child has all the talent and tools to become a superstar just because he can shoot ten baskets in a row and clearly outshines his peers. Such a notion is absurd. Children mature physically and athletically at different paces. What you can ensure is that your child has the opportunity to develop a strong athletic foundation in an age-appropriate setting. That way you provide him with the proper nourishment to grow his talent and maximize his athletic potential.

Play/sports development is broken up into four main stages:

1. Stage One: five- to eight-year-olds

2. Stage Two: nine- to eleven-year-olds

3. Stage Three: twelve- to fifteen-year-olds

4. Stage Four: sixteen- to eighteen-year-olds

Stage One: Balance and Coordination

In this stage, children ages five to eight are taught engaging games that help develop their movement skills (e.g., running and jumping), balance, and coordination, and they are given ample time and space to continue to play freely. Sport-specific skills are not taught at this stage. Once or twice a week a mini-Olympics composed of games that encourage movement, experimentation, and creativity can be set up. These are not outcome-oriented games. The emphasis is on fun and skill development. We strongly recommend home sports schooling for this age group. In chapter 6 we offer specifics, providing examples of backyard and park activities that help develop balance and movement skills, and creative thinking (also see activities in chapter 4).

Stage Two: Fundamental Skills

During the nine- to eleven-year-old stage, sport-specific skills like catching, throwing, and kicking are incorporated into movement and balance training. Self-measuring competitions can help keep kids excited and engaged as they practice fundamental skills. We find that they enjoy measuring and tracking their own progress. Traditional sports games, which are the norm at this age level, often take up too much time and detract from the development of fundamental skills. Kids should be engaged, not milling about on the sidelines waiting for their turn to play.

We recommend that traditional sports games be introduced at a later age, after the fundamentals have been taught and practiced for several years. Basic introduction to team play begins with games that are adapted to suit the age group. For example, football is introduced as flag football; soccer is presented in three vs. three format; ice hockey and lacrosse are taught in smaller playing areas (not full-size arenas or fields), with rules adapted to suit the space configuration and age group (see activities in chapters 4 and 6).

Stage Three: Sport-Specific Techniques

At the twelve- to fifteen-year-old stage, children are taught more complex sport-specific techniques like turning a double play, executing a corner kick, or blocking and tackling. They experiment at different positions, work on the interpretation of rules, and are introduced to game strategy. They also continue to take part in short-sided, small-space games and self-measuring skill competitions. Children should play a different sport each season at this stage, as it is still too early to introduce year-round specialization, which is detrimental to well-rounded athletic development. The negative effects of early specialization far outweigh any perceived advantages, as is poignantly underscored in *Until It Hurts,* Mark Hyman's study of pushy sports parents and their physically and emotionally damaged children (see activities in chapters 7 and 8).

Stage Four: Training and Competing

The final stage—ages sixteen to eighteen—is an exciting time for the well-rounded athlete. She now has well-developed movement skills, experience playing multiple sports, and a high level of proficiency in sport-specific skills (like skating, passing, and shooting in hockey). With such a strong, basic physical and cognitive foundation, she can adapt her athletic skills to any sport(s) and is ready to train and compete in regulation-size playing spaces (fields, courts, rinks) in full-size games. The training focus should continue to be on developing sport- and position-specific techniques through drills and small-sided, small-space games. Then she can be tested and hone her skills in regulation-size competitive team play (see activities in chapters 7 and 8).

We urge parents and sports educators to study how kids learn by observing action-sports athletes. Visit a skate park or mountain half-pipe. Note the activities and interactions of the young athletes who train there. They gather without a pre-scheduled practice time or designated coach. They confer with each other, and no matter what their skill level, ability, or age, they coach each other. Everyone is focused on practicing the execution of fundamentals. Most important: They are all having fun. As Olympic gold medalist snowboarder Hannah Teter says, "We progress faster as athletes because we are having fun, which is the key to success in any sport." In fact, every action-sports athlete we've ever talked to, male or female, has echoed skateboarder Ryan Sheckler's sentiments: "It's not about winning. Winning happens when you are having fun. If you are not having fun and your head's not into it, what's the point?"

The proof is in the passion. Skateboarders and snowboarders spend not hours or days, but months—years, even—developing and perfecting one technical aspect of a challenging trick. What drives such passion for practice? What fuels such dedication to work over and over to achieve fundamental improvement? Can we infuse organized sports with the same focus and intention? The answer is yes! We can invigorate organized sports by providing kids with a place and space in which they have the freedom to self-discover and develop new skills, a place where peer mentorship is nurtured and adult guidance is appropriately limited.

Taking a page from the action-sports paradigm, we have designed an athletic development program that can be implemented at home and in your neighborhood. All you need is access to one or more of these resources:

1. At home: backyards, driveways, basements

2. In public parks: fields, courts, open spaces

3. At organized community events throughout your child's play and sports experience

The following chapters will show you how to create a well-rounded approach in your home and beyond, so that your children can thrive and improve their skills while you manage their time and yours more productively. This is not about going "back to basics" in some idealized past. We *value* the basics as we look forward to a more balanced sports environment for children. That's what Whole Child Sports strives to achieve.

CHAPTER 2

Your Sports Biography—
Does It Hinder or Help?

We've all seen it: The ranting parent who stalks the sidelines, fuming at a blown call or a missed shot. Poised to pounce on anyone and everyone in his field of vision, he settles on the most vulnerable of targets, his own son. Out comes a laundry list of perceived mistakes and failures. As the subject of this public humiliation cowers, trying to shrink into his Little League uniform, the rest of us recoil at the sight of a child distressed by the person he most eagerly wishes to please: his dad.

But the truth is that there is likely something of an ogre in all of us. Somewhere in America, on any given day, any one of us can fly into a rage, convinced that our child has been purposefully slighted, injured, or mistreated, or that he isn't giving it his all on the field, in spite of the fact that we just spent four hours and $300 driving him to a weekend tournament in Sportsville.

In this chapter we examine why parents can become so vested in their children's athletic success that they dampen their kids' sports experiences. We'll answer questions parents have asked us and provide practical psychological techniques we can all use to avoid falling into the trap of identifying too closely

with our children's performance. We've found that when parents mine the depth of their personal sports biographies, they can embrace the positive experiences they've had and come to terms with the unpleasant ones. We tend to project our anxieties and expectations on our children. If we learn to be more mindful of our influence over them, we can give them the space to experience the joys and challenges of sports in their own unique way.

Your Sports History Influences Your Child

If we want to create a more wholesome sports experience for our children—a time of joy, fun, and learning—the first step is to try to understand our own sports biographies and how they may be influencing our kids' experiences. In *Parenting from the Inside Out,* Dr. Dan Siegel points out that when we become parents, "we bring with us issues from our own past that influence the way we parent our children." So it stands to reason that unresolved issues from our childhood sports experiences can, and often do, trigger some pretty curious, unfortunate, and maybe even outrageous sideline antics.

Let's not play the blame game. We've all done or said things we regret at one time or another. The three of us certainly have, even though we've coached kids for decades. What all of us can do is be proactive—work hard to prepare for the next time we are about to lose it. Literally. We can discover what triggers us and why, and in understanding ourselves better we will most certainly take the edge off such moments of "temporary insanity." What better behavior to model for our kids than our hard-won sideline self-control?

When taken at face value, overblown emotional reactions, distorted perceptions, and unbecoming impulse behaviors make little sense, but they are common at youth sports events. So what if your nine-year-old missed a penalty shot? Did that really give you license to kick the cooler over and toss your cap a dozen feet into the bushes? Each of us can do something to take the sting out of our occasionally outlandish behavior. We can get to know ourselves a little better and take responsibility for our outbursts by trying to identify the root causes of our behavior. Our kids will love us for it, because when we lose control we embarrass them deeply. If they see that we are learning to keep our cool, they will feel intense relief and appreciation, and may even learn to take things in stride themselves.

Thomas and Alice Brommer learned the hard way that their daughter, Lisa, is wilting under the pressure of parental expectations. An Olympic-caliber swimmer at sixteen, Lisa's times are so good that she is looking at a scholarship to her pick of the top college programs in the United States. Thomas, her dad, is ecstatic. He's been her number one fan since her Tadpole days. Though a corporate tax lawyer with a frenetic work schedule, he's been a fixture at early morning practices and weekend meets.

Lisa's mom, Alice, on the other hand, is worried. Two years ago Lisa suffered from a severe case of chronic fatigue syndrome triggered by overtraining. She was forced to stop swimming for an entire year. Now signs of a potential relapse have surfaced. Lisa is overtraining again. She's tired all the time, and cranky and abrasive, not her usual sunny self. What's worse, Lisa has always been a straight A student, but suddenly her grades have nosedived. She's acting out, talking back to her mother, and hanging out with a seedy crowd. A couple of the boys are particularly unsavory, and Lisa seems to always be with them when she's not in the pool.

But what pushes Alice over the edge is the day she discovers that Lisa has branded herself. Not just with one tattoo, but three. The row at the kitchen table is apocalyptic. Yelling and screaming give way to slammed doors and a river of tears. That night—when things have settled down a bit—Alice and Thomas talk about the stranger now occupying their daughter's bedroom. Alice is stunned by the changes she's witnessed in her little girl. Thomas, ever the pragmatist, concludes that Lisa's poor judgment and moodiness are symptomatic of adolescent angst. He counsels patience.

Alice is not so sure. She calls her older sister, Liz, a doting aunt with a grating habit of blurting out unfiltered truths. "You know how much I admire Thomas, honey," Liz says, "but he's got to be the source of all this craziness. Lisa loves him to death, and she's been trying to impress him since forever. She's probably reached her breaking point." As Alice hangs up the phone, it all clicks. Lisa's reluctance to get out of bed. Her fatigue. Her sullen attitude. It suddenly all makes sense. The pressure she places on herself to be the best has been fueled by not wanting to let down her dad. And it's sinking her.

Still, Alice is loath to approach Thomas. He's never bought into the chronic fatigue diagnosis. He believes that Lisa is shirking her responsibilities and squandering her athletic potential. She simply needs to toughen up a bit. He was a brilliant breast stroker in college, with elite-level times, and he knows what it takes to compete: work, dedication, and sheer willpower. He had all three in spades but had to shelve his national team aspirations when Alice got pregnant with Lisa. He took the responsible route and went to law school. To complicate matters further, Alice knows that swimming has always been the bridge that binds father and daughter. It's the foundation upon which their relationship is built.

A few weeks later Alice is jarred into action. Lisa has hit rock bottom. The dreaded call from school comes: She's been caught binge drinking behind the gym at a dance. That night Alice lays it all on the line. "This is a disaster, Thomas," she says. "We're losing Lisa. This is our daughter's life, not yours. You cannot make her live your life."

Alice and Thomas meet with Lisa and tell her they think she should take a break from swimming. Her eyes well up. She hugs her parents, overwhelmed by relief. She feels a tremendous weight lifted off her shoulders. And she quits cold turkey. For the next eight months Lisa steers clear of any and every pool. Then, without any prompting from her dad or coach, she jumps back in. She falls in love with training and competing again, and decides to pursue her Olympic dream. Within six months she is posting her best times ever.

Lisa's story has a happy ending. Alice realized that her daughter needed time away from swimming, and Thomas finally saw that he had been pushing her too hard for years. He had inadvertently contaminated her sports experience. They backed off before it was too late. However, most parents do not. Stories like Lisa's play out across America each year at every level of every sport. The result: Seventy percent of children quit youth sports by the age of thirteen. The top two reasons they cite? Parents and coaches, who are often critical or push too hard.

The Self-Reflective Sports Parent

In order to get to know your own sports biography and become aware of how it may be influencing your child's sports experience, ask yourself these ten questions:

1. What were my parents' attitudes toward sports and my involvement? Were they involved? Pushy? Disinterested? How did their attitude make me feel?

2. What were my worst childhood sports experiences? Why?

3. What were my best youth sports experiences? Why?

4. Does my past athletic success or failure change the way I feel about how my child should approach her involvement in sports?

5. Why did we put our child into sports? What do we hope he will get out of this experience? Does he want to play, or is it mostly us wanting him to play? Are our goals for him realistic?

6. What's my reaction when I read about or witness over-the-top parents at games?

7. Can I take a step back? Is this situation or event really that important to my child's future success and happiness?

8. What memories would I like my child to have about me when she reflects on her sports experiences with her own kids?

9. What would my child want me to do right now in this situation?

10. Will this situation I'm getting so worked up about really matter twenty-four hours from now?

Why Am I So Critical After My Child's Game?

I often find myself angry and critical after watching my son play a soccer game and catch myself becoming really judgmental and negative about the coaches and referees—and even my own son. Why is this happening?

Discussion: First off, you can breathe easy. You are not alone. Many people experience this. A University of Maryland study found that 53 percent of parents surveyed after watching their children play soccer reported being angry during games to some degree. The most frequently cited irritants were referees (35 percent) and their own child or their child's team (28 percent).

A lot of this can come from unresolved issues from our past. While these normally sit just under the surface, when it's about our kids, and they are interacting dynamically with other kids, something primal in us is touched that goes very deep. Let's not kid ourselves. Seeing our children play sports with other children is something that can provide the greatest pleasure and the greatest pain. It can be a raw, instinctual experience. When we descend into that place, a lot of our own unresolved issues are unearthed. Our kids take us there. It's why parenting is the most amazing path. But in sports, they take us there quickly. Being a sports parent offers us a great opportunity to become conscious about what's going on with our own emotions, and it's a lot cheaper than therapy.

One parent we spoke to says he has trouble restraining himself from criticizing his son when he makes mistakes in a game, and when they go to the park to play catch or basketball, his son gets frustrated and wants to quit early. When the dad took a hard look at what was going on, he realized that rather than having fun with his boy, he spent the entire outing "instructing" him on how to execute a layup or throw a ball properly, analyzing his every move. That's why it had become a chore for the child.

When the dad reviewed his own childhood, he realized that the reason he pressured his son so much and wanted him to play flawlessly could be traced back to his own father's pitting him against his siblings in competitions all the time. "There was no horsing around," he says. "There was always an agenda." Everything was regimented and outcome based. The dad now understands that his anxiety about his son's performance was rooted in his own childhood insecurities.

Solution: The best way to break that generational pattern is to become aware of it, and then pay attention and catch yourself when you have the impulse to interfere with your child's sports experience. You may feel compelled to say something judgmental about your child's performance, or about the coach or referee. At that moment, you can apply what we call the three-heartbeat rule. It used to be called the "count to ten" rule, but, as you know, the pace of life has changed, so three heartbeats will do. Ask yourself three simple questions before you say anything:

1. Is it true?

2. Is it kind?

3. Is it necessary?

You might answer, "It *is* true! He made a lousy pass. He's not even trying that hard." But then you come up against, "Is it kind?" Most often the answer is no. And is it necessary? Is it strictly necessary? Almost never. Ask yourself what you will achieve by criticizing. In most cases, once you've answered these three questions, you will decide to resist the impulse to make the comment.

The feedback we are getting from the tens of thousands of people in the *Simplicity Parenting* movement (which grew out of Kim's first book of the same name) who practice this simple exercise in their daily lives is very positive. What we hear over and over is that when they reflect later, they feel proud and pleased with themselves. They were able to hold back. That's a big thing. That restraint has helped them to be better parents, better partners, and better work colleagues. This is not just a sports lesson—it's a life lesson.

Know Your Triggers

In addition to knowing how your own sports biography can affect your child's youth sports experience, it's also important to know what triggers you when you watch your child participate in sports. Triggers are those things that quickly—almost instantly—cause you to become angry or upset when your child is playing and can result in negative behavior. Some of the most common sports parent anger triggers are:

- Seeing your child get injured
- Disagreeing with referee calls
- Believing that the coach is mistreating your child

- Objecting to the way another parent treats your kid
- Thinking that your child is underperforming and not trying hard enough
- Feeling jealous when your child's teammates experience success on the field

The Most Common Underlying Reasons Parents Overreact When Their Kids Play Sports

1. We see athletics as a way to overcome economic hardship (scholarship seekers).

2. We are overcome by anxiety over whether our child will be competitive and tough enough to succeed in life.

3. We want our kids to succeed where we failed on the field of play.

4. We have a burning desire for our children to follow in our footsteps and replicate our perceived success in a specific sport.

5. We feel vulnerable and exposed when our kids perform or underperform in public. We see our children as extensions of ourselves. We take it personally.

6. We have unresolved emotional wounds stemming from our own experiences in youth sports.

7. We become frustrated when our kids fail to mimic the stylized movements of pro athletes we see on television, though they are clearly not yet physically capable of doing so. They just can't move that way yet.

It's helpful to know your triggers, because once you know exactly what they are, you can more easily learn how to defuse your anger and respond more appropriately in any given situation.

De-Triggering: Navigating Emotional Land Mines

Part of learning how to recognize your triggers and defuse them is also knowing how your own sports biography sometimes sparks these triggers. Once you are aware of how your history affects your current perceptions and feelings, you can more easily identify when that is the real reason you are reacting and instead focus on the present and your child's situation. The following are four methods to strip your comments of biographical undertones.

1. **Talk less; listen more.** Be a witness and supporter. You don't need to be a sportscaster parent. Cut the number of times you speak up by 50 percent. Then cut that in half again. Really . . . half, then half again.

2. **Say what you see.** If you have to talk, say what you see. "The team really picked it up in the second quarter. You guys were moving the ball really well and tightened up defensively. Yeah, what I saw was that . . . "

3. **Ask a question.** Ask a question rather than making a statement. For example, if you feel your child wasn't giving it his best, don't say, "It didn't look like you were giving it your best out there," or "You were really

dogging it." Instead try something like, "Did you feel a bit tired today?"

4. **Frame your comments carefully.** Remember to recount your child's genuine and often subtle successes. Don't criticize *or* overpraise him. Something simple and focused like, "Boy, that time you fell over and still got up quickly and got back on defense really seemed to help," sets just the right tone.

One Parent's Golden Moment

Sports push us to the brink, and when we stand on the edge of that precipice, all charged up with purpose and passion, the unexpected happens: a golden moment. We've asked everyone from recreational-league enthusiasts to accomplished athletes to share their golden sports moments. Surprisingly, these recollections rarely resemble anything you'd associate with a highlight reel: a game winning three-pointer, a grand slam home run, or an overtime goal scored. Instead, they're almost always about friendships, relationships, and the connections made, about the people who supported them when times were tough, encouraged them to face their challenges, and helped them learn and grow.

During a recent parenting workshop, a former NCAA Division I running back stood up to share his golden moment. Everyone expected to hear about a stirring nationally televised victory or a thirty-yard breakthrough touchdown run. But instead, as this hulking man teared up, he too spoke about connection and second chances.

College had been a difficult time for him. In high school he was a superstar, and everything had come easily. On the field and off he'd been successful and immensely popular. Now, on a bigger stage, away from family and friends, things fell apart. He underperformed on the field and in the classroom, and the failure he'd never experienced before gnawed away at his insides. In practice he had difficulty following the complex new playbook. He missed openings, misread the defense, and dropped easy passes. Angry and frustrated, he acted out. There were shoving arguments with other players, smashed lockers, and flipped massage tables. His bad attitude and childish locker room antics caught the attention of his coaches, and an argument was made for cutting him from the team.

"My coach could have cut me," he recalls. "I'd given him ample reason." Instead the coach separated the behavior from the being. He saw the core person, whose pain was stifling his potential, and he talked to the boy. Counseled him. He reprimanded him repeatedly for his misbehavior and set boundaries. "You can't act that way," he said. "You're better than that!" This mixture of firmness and acceptance made all the difference.

There is nothing worse than being judged by your behavior when it is at its most raw and unresolved. To have someone look beyond it is an amazing gift.

The lesson and values this coach taught this player live on in his own parenting: "Being treated that way gave me the ability to look beyond my boy's tantrums and bad behavior. I still say, 'Hey! You can't behave that way.' But I don't get caught up in the raw emotion. I tell him, 'You're better than that. Something else is going on. No. Don't shout and scream. Tell me what's up.' It's made all the difference."

Discover Your Golden Moment

Shift your focus. Stand on the bedrock of healthy experience rather than the thin ice of unresolved past experiences:

Pause. Think about and recall a golden moment from your own play, game, or sports experience. A beautiful, uncomplicated memory. Picture it in your mind. Dwell in it and savor it.

Then describe it. Think of three reasons why it was golden. For example, was it the moment a friendship was made? Was it because someone took time with you or maybe someone recognized your sincere efforts even though you lost the game?

Think about how you can help create such an experience for your child. Can you help build such memories for your kids? Can you help them to build their own memories by being present and creating opportunities for them to experience their own golden moments?

Why Are We So Overprotective Today?

Playing through pain was the way we did things when I was a kid. It defined us as men. We paraded our toughness with pride. Nowadays everyone seems overprotective. I played youth football myself. Am I supposed to wrap my child up in bubble wrap? I survived. Why shouldn't he?

Discussion: In the past we participated in youth sports somewhat blindly, assuming that the full contact in football or hockey, and repeated heading of the ball in soccer, had no lasting physical impact on children. Manliness or toughness in general was defined as an ability to play through pain. Our heroes were players who sacrificed their bodies to the altar of victory.

Today we are armed with a plethora of scientific knowledge that has turned that mythology on its head. Your child is not heroic because he takes another snap after having his "bell rung." He's at risk, and there may be far-reaching, long-term consequences. If you let him play through such an injury, you are seen by even-keeled folk not so much as the proud parent of a warrior child, but as one who willfully puts his child in harm's way.

What we know about concussions and overuse injuries today has redefined the way we look at tenacity and toughness in youth sports. With all the information out there about the long-term effects of concussions and certain serious joint injuries (like torn ACLs), we have become wiser about potential problems.

One can argue that all this information has also made us nervous, anxious, and perhaps overly protective. Sports inherently involve contact. Kids will always be banging into each other when they play. We cannot avoid contact in youth sports, but we can certainly be much more proactive about injury prevention, now that we are armed with so much detailed information about the nature of injuries.

It's important to realize that we often romanticize the past. The following are three comments we hear all too often:

1. "That's not the way I was taught."

2. "That's not the way I played the game."

3. "That's not the way it's played by the pros."

Such attitudes may cloud our vision. Few people knew better when we were children, and the pros we watch on television are adults, not kids. Their bodies and brains are fully formed. They can handle a level of strain and stress that children cannot. When kids play adult versions of sports like hockey and football, they check hard and tackle each other the way the pros do. On YouTube you can watch videos of eight- and nine-year-old kids engaged in full-impact helmet-to-helmet clashes, egged on by cheering parents. These adults may get their thrills watching little kids do what the pros do and boast about their tykes' toughness, but they must be oblivious to the damage these actions may be doing to their children's developing brains and bodies.

Solution: We have to ask ourselves point-blank: Is the risk worth the outcome? There is enough information available now to clarify what the risks are. There are also alternative ways children can learn and play games like football and hockey that are safer than the adult-centric version we learned back in the day. To be clear, we are not suggesting you take your child out of organized football or hockey if he is at the right age and developmental stage to play. And we don't advocate being "soft" with kids. They'll get bumps, scrapes, and bruises when they play sports. That's fine. It's expected. But there are ways to teach kids the fundamentals of certain sports without endangering their bodies and brains. These sports do not have to be taught or played the way they were when we were children. There is a clear distinction between soft and safe. We have good information now on the dangers of certain activities, and the responsible thing is to err on the side of caution.

Mainstream youth sports organizations have finally begun to adjust the way kids play sports—given the deluge of research data on head injuries in sports. The stubbornly old-school mind-set about toughness is being replaced by a more cautious, pragmatic approach. In 2011, USA Hockey eliminated body checking in their twelve-and-under youth divisions. And starting in 2012, Pop Warner football (the nation's largest youth football league) set limits on the frequency of full-contact practice drills. Even some Division I college football programs have cut down on contact drills in practices. A Red Bulls youth soccer coach we spoke with says he no longer incorporates full-on header practice in his youth training programs. When he does teach heading techniques, he uses NERF or beach balls. That way kids can avoid the severe headaches that can come from the repeated heading of regulation-size soccer balls during practice drills.

Much more needs to be done to make sports safer for our kids, but to begin with, we have to become more aware of the dangers. In their seminal book *Concussions and Our Kids: America's Leading Expert on How to Protect Young Athletes and Keep Sports Safe,* Dr. Robert Cantu and coauthor Mark Hyman focus on what has become a veritable epidemic in youth sports: the prevalence of concussions. "Concussions happen to all types of athletes—young and old, boys and girls, and in every conceivable sport," Cantu warns. "[They occur] when an athlete is slammed and makes sudden and forceful contact. That contact can be with the ground, court or pool deck. It can also be with a batted ball, a thrown ball, a kicked ball, a goalpost (football), the boards (hockey), the scorer's table (basketball), and of course another player." Parents should arm themselves with information about sports safety, from books like Cantu's, so that they can both be proactive in keeping their children out of harm's way and know precisely what to do to protect and help them recover quickly and fully, should they suffer a head trauma.

Does It Matter if I Don't Have a Sports History?

I'm worried that my lack of experience and success in sports is going to bias my child's sports experience. I don't feel very confident about coaching or guiding him. What should I do?

Discussion: Most first-time sports parents are insecure about being their child's primary coach. But the simple truth is that you know your child better than anyone else. You've been there since day one, watched him take his first steps and held him through the night when he was sick, so no one knows him individually better than you do. Take advantage of that knowledge. Guide him in the manner you know is best for him, learn alongside him—and keep things light and fun.

The mistake we often make is that we try to compare ourselves with master coaches. There are very few people at that level. Even the best youth coaches are constantly learning on the job about their specialty sport, about dealing with individual children, and about navigating group dynamics. Between the three of us, we've taught thousands of hours of gymnastics, soccer, basketball, and football, among other sports, yet we are frequently stumped and have to reconfigure practices, adapt approaches, and incorporate ideas cribbed from other coaches' practice plans or experience.

Whole Child Sports is about engagement, not outcome. We noticed a mom in a park recently, playing football with her two young sons. She was wearing street clothes and cumbersome heels—not exactly the type of attire we recommend when you are playing with your kids. She was also possibly the world's worst quarterback. Her passes were wobbly and often underthrown. But two things trumped such glaring defects:

She was trying, and her kids were having an awesome time. They ran, leapt, and dodged with as much alacrity and intensity as they would have in any Pop Warner football training session.

Solution: Stay engaged. That's the key. If you remain involved, you encourage your child to remain active and build your relationship with her. Kids crave connection; they value it over expertise. And who knows? The fact that you don't know so much about sports may encourage your child to take greater ownership of her experience. If you don't know how to execute a layup, you can look it up in a book with her. Discover the answer together, or find someone who knows and learn alongside him or her. Don't just hand your kid over to a coach.

This bears repeating: Get involved and stay connected to the process. As your child learns and advances, you can ask him to teach you what he is learning. Showing you how it's done does wonders for his confidence. If you are a bit squeamish about undermining your own authority, think of it this way: By the age of ten, most kids have figured out that their parents don't know it all, anyway. So it's okay to say, "You know what? I never really played golf. You did it at school? Wow. Teach me what you learned about making a putt."

Take pleasure in your child's exploration. It's her discovery. Your engagement is what matters, not your proficiency. Have her teach you the rules. The key is not to pretend. Be honest with her. You don't have to learn the sport yourself. You may want to, or you may not. That's fine. Just spend the time with her. Listen to her and enjoy her exploration. You will not lose credibility if you care and take the time. She will become the teacher and learn by showing you.

In fact, you often travel lighter when you have no sports baggage. In our experience, some of the best sports parents are moms and dads who don't know the sport their children play, but support them and spend time with them. The lack of a sports biography can be a striking positive. Without experience in the sport, parents can focus more on supporting their kids, rather than expending energy trying to second-guess coaches and referees. Your ignorance becomes a sports-parenting plus.

The kids have made it quite clear: They want you at their games, but only if you are going to sit quietly and watch them play. What do they think about know-it-all parents who can't help but speak out? Well, they responded in a survey conducted by *Sports Illustrated for Kids* on "The Top Ten Things Parents Don't Get About Sports," and here are our top three picks:

1. "I hate when parents tell us to do the exact opposite of what the coaches say."

2. "Parents think they know the rules, but they don't."

3. And our favorite: "Parents who yell and scream look like dorks."

Why Shouldn't We Want to Win at All Costs?

I've always thought sports were about winning. That's what I was taught. That's why we keep score. Now I'm told kids can be successful without winning, and everybody gets a trophy. Other parents seem really comfortable with that. My kids are like me. They want to win. We feel bad when we lose. Where do we fit in?

Discussion: You seem to be the type of person who sets high personal goals, and that's good. You are not easy on yourself. You are motivated and have high expectations. That's okay, too. But you bring up an extremely important issue in youth sports: the narrow focus on outcome. Let's start by trying to expand the term *winning*. The truth is that final results are reductive. The game is over. The score was 5–2. One team won; the other lost. End of story. Right? Well, no. Not really. Winning is definitely important, but the final score is too narrow an indicator for success. Our obsession with final results can mislead us.

We have found that the most successful coaches, teams, and programs are driven by different principles of success. Winning is a by-product of their efforts, not the main focus. Top-level coaches break down success and failure. They look hard at wins and losses to see what was done well and what wasn't. Then they build practices around this information. It's a basic educational principle: You recognize your team's weaknesses and work on them, and you celebrate its strengths and build on them.

As a society we don't celebrate mistakes enough. In fact, we often cower from them. But mistakes and losses provide a solid foundation for growth and long-term improvement, which should be our ultimate goal. Perhaps legendary UCLA basketball coach John Wooden put it best: "Let's face it, we are all imperfect, and we are going to fall short on occasion. But we must learn from failure, and that will enable us to avoid repeating our mistakes. Through adversity, we learn, grow stronger, and become better people."

Kids play sports for two reasons: to have fun and to learn. If their primary focus is on "winning at all costs," they will have difficulty enjoying themselves, win or lose. The pressure they feel ultimately deflates their enthusiasm. When the fun's gone, thoughts of quitting loom large.

Learning has an even weaker correlation with winning. Let's break this down so that when you watch a game you can see that your daughter's key successes actually have very little to do with the final score. She's a developing athlete, so if her team loses 5–0 but she's made some really good passes or fired off her first-ever shot on goal, she's had a superb game. She's a winner. There are myriad ways to define individual success during a game, none of which directly relates to the outcome. If your child improved his shot percentage, or made more assists than ever before, or gained good yardage for the first time, these are major victories and should be celebrated as such.

The truth is we cannot control final results. We can influence them by practicing hard and playing with zest, but a bad call or an untimely injury can change the outcome in a split second. What matters much more are the lessons that are being learned by the children playing these games. And remember, they are games—just games. Kids are at play here. They are learning and developing skills and, we hope, positive character traits. But they are not defined by what the scoreboard flashes when time has elapsed. They are defined by what they've learned, how much effort they've put in, and how they behave on the field and after the game.

Solution: It's perfectly fine to talk about winning and losing, and to think about the final score. Please don't misunderstand us. The outcome is an integral part of the game. But it's also important to step back and realize that the final score is really only one aspect of winning. Effort exerted, execution of skills, and behavior on the field are of equal importance in measuring a complete victory.

In our experience with sports parenting, when you recognize the various levels of winning and losing, it will almost certainly help you feel comfortable at your daughter's games. You can score her game differently. Focus on her individual effort and keep track of her passes, shots, or great defensive plays. Basically, you can create a mental highlight reel of your kid's individual successes on the court and later in the day play them back to her, but not necessarily right after the game. Give her some breathing room. Then later you can say, "You know, I noticed you were doing the pick-and-roll your coach taught you really well this morning. I saw you do it five times in the third quarter. I've never seen you do it so well before."

By doing this, you make it clear to your child that:

- You pay close attention at her games.
- You place much more value on the fact that she's making efforts and learning than on the fact that her team lost 56–47.
- Your definition of success is directly related to her individual efforts and work within the team, and not tied to something that's completely out of her control: the final outcome.

Let's put this into perspective: Kids forget outcomes quickly. Win or lose, they move on. But what they do remember—sometimes for decades—is if you overemphasize winning and your negative reactions to their losses.

Take a Cue from Your Kids: One Parent's Eye-Opening Travel Team Trip

I want to share an experience I had with my son Tommy's U12 basketball team, which really put things in perspective for all of us.

On a hot summer weekend in June, a group of thirty of us—Hawks players, parents, and coaches—drove to the Jersey Shore to play in an Amateur Athletic Union (AAU) round-robin tournament. Our boys were a tightly knit group of skilled, well-coached players who were used to winning games, so it came as no surprise that they won their first two on Saturday, putting them just one victory shy of qualifying for the Sunday semi-finals. Saturday evening's game was a nail-biter, though, and at the end of regulation we were deadlocked at 44–44.

To conclude games quickly, tournament organizers had to concoct an unusual overtime (OT) scheme: Two minutes were allotted for the first overtime, and, if needed, the second overtime would be sudden death: The first team to score wins.

At the end of the first OT the game was still tied, so we braced ourselves for the all-important tip-off to start the second OT. The Hawks had been winning tip-offs all season, so we were quite confident as the ball was tossed into the air. We were shocked by what happened next. Our opponents won the tip-off and in a matter of seconds scored an easy layup to win the game. Final score: 48–46. Our kids were stunned. In a flash the tournament was over for them: no Sunday playoffs.

It took all of five minutes for the kids to put this disheartening loss behind them. The chorus of questions that ensued instantly clarified their reshuffled priorities: "When do we get to the pool?" "Can we order pizza?" "Can we watch the Celtics game tonight?" There were no long faces or watery eyes. The kids had moved on.

Now, their parents—that was a different story. Many were visibly upset. They couldn't stop replaying the game's outcome. Hours later, at dinner, they were still rehashing it, complaining about the referee and harping on the unusual sudden death overtime set up. The kids, who were seated at the opposite end of the table, were oblivious to this discussion.

Then one mom spoke up. "Look at the kids," she said. "They haven't said a word about the loss since game time. They have a much healthier perspective than we do."

Create an Alternative Narrative: A Different Way to Score Your Child's Game

We all have stories from our personal sports biographies, and that's fine, but as parents our deep wish should be that our kids develop their own stories. You can create a whole new narrative: your kid's most treasured and enduring memories. As you string together the top ten moments in your kid's game, keep in mind that they don't all have to be about the goal he scored or the shot she saved. Included among them can be unexpected gems. For example, that 1,000-watt smile you caught on your daughter's face as she started the final kick of her 800-meter race, or the perfect, selfless pass that your son made when he had a clear shot at the goal but noticed a teammate in better scoring position.

The following are four specific ways that you can better respond to your young athlete's game:

1. Hold your criticism.

2. Create an alternative narrative by developing a mental highlight reel of your kid's game and playing it back to him over the next few days.

3. Keep your comments simple and focused. Don't shower your child with false praise. It embarrasses her.

4. Remember: What you say matters. Really matters. There are no throwaway comments, so be careful and be prepared.

This is the Whole Child Sports approach in practice. Because, by including positive comments about her *whole* performance, you are, in effect, saying to your child, "I'm present, and I notice all of you—not just the points or goals you score." A kid thrives when basking in the glow of her parents' attention. With this approach you avoid being a hovering sports critic or fan whom she worries about impressing but are a parent, first and foremost, and a partner, someone who accepts her and with whom she shares these special moments on her athletic journey. That's how you develop a Whole Child.

CHAPTER 3

Too Much, Too Soon

Like millions of American boys, Joey Smith dreamed of becoming a professional baseball player. He started out at five with T-ball and played year-round. Joey ate, breathed, and slept baseball, and as he grew bigger and stronger, he started turning heads at tournaments and all-star games.

On the field, the results were nothing short of remarkable. By age eleven, Joey was striking out batters in bunches. The shutouts piled up, and trophies lined every shelf in the Smith household. While neither of his parents had ever been interested in sports growing up—mom was a musician and dad an architect—they were thrilled to see their son excel at something he loved to do. Admittedly, they were downright proud of all the attention they received as parents of the town team's star.

The Smiths were model sports parents—or so it seemed. They never raised their voices at games and were always positive with Joey and supportive of the team. But due to their lack of sports experience, they deferred to Joey's team coaches on all things baseball. The coaches were the experts, they figured, and boy, did the coaches love Joey! He was modest, enthusiastic, and a hard worker, and he made them look good. Really good. They happily devoted a lot of free time to working with him, grooming him during special workouts and extra training sessions.

With Joey on the mound, regional titles were within reach. It was exciting and a win-win situation for everyone involved—except Joey. No one bothered to check in with him. Not his parents, who thought everything was peachy, nor his coaches, who were doing what they'd always done when presented with a naturally gifted kid with a golden arm: mold the boy into a championship-caliber pitcher.

If any of them had been more attentive, they might have realized that Joey was tired. Exhausted, really. The constant training and playing for five years was taking its toll on his little body, and as his practice days grew longer and more workmanlike, the down time during which he could pursue other interests or simply horse around evaporated. The walls started to close in.

However, no one noticed the change, including Joey, until it got really bad. Joey started complaining about stomachaches and faking injuries so he could skip practice and stay home, so he could hang out and not worry about his pitching mechanics or winning games.

On the days his dad drove him to practice, he'd ask if they could park the car all the way on the other side of the river, ten minutes by foot from the ballpark, instead of in the parking lot right next to the field. He cherished these walks with his dad. He'd race down to the river to skip stones for a few minutes, until his dad called out that they'd be late for practice. Soon several of his teammates joined in. Picture a cluster of kids in baseball uniforms horsing around, skipping rocks by the river before practice.

The trouble for Joey was that—like any other kid his age—his self-worth was all tangled up in his pitching persona. As he grew better and better, he became addicted to the attention he received from his coaches and teammates. He internalized the pressure to perform at a high level, so eager to please everyone that he lost any sense of himself and what he wanted to do. Like many budding American athletes, Joey was a competitive kid who specialized in the sport he loved at too young and impressionable an age.

No one stepped in to put on the brakes, to call an occasional time-out, or to make sure there were other activities in Joey's life to provide him with a healthy dose of diverse experiences. With such guidance he could have developed a better balance between baseball and everything else a little kid should explore as he grows up and becomes a young man.

The extent to which Joey retreated from the pressures of his "profession" are astounding. He began to fantasize that his dad had crashed the family car on the way to practice. He envisioned them hitting a telephone pole and being injured so badly that they were hospitalized. He imagined having his dad all to himself as they lay in adjacent beds in a recovery room, conjuring up extensive uninterrupted conversations they'd have in their one-on-one time together.

For Joey things did not end happily, at least not from a sports perspective. During his eleventh year he quit baseball.

Everyone was shocked, but for him it was the only way to quell the overwhelming fear he had of failing, of drowning in everyone's disappointment. He joined the 70 percent of American youths who had quit organized sports by the age of thirteen: young teenagers who turned their backs on youth sports at precisely the age when they were physically, emotionally, and socially primed to benefit from the experience of training and playing in the challenging, competitive, socially dynamic context that individual and team sports can and should provide.

Today's win-at-all-costs culture subjects children like Joey to too much, too soon. Starting at age five or six (sometimes even younger), children are pressured to perform by parents, coaches, and, more insidiously, by societal attitudes disseminated by overzealous media marketers. Success is packaged so cleverly that children are unable to avoid internalizing the belief that their self-worth is inextricably linked to short-term success.

At Whole Child Sports we want to slow things down a bit for these youngsters, to give kids the time and space to develop properly, at a more reasonable pace. We recognize that each child's life unfolds at its own unique, subjective pace and that kids can thrive and reach their full potential as athletes and adults if they are taught in developmentally appropriate stages. That's why we emphasize the benefits of free play and loosely structured skill-building activities in the younger years. That's why we encourage parents to learn to temper their overt and subconscious influences on their child's sports experience. As kids grow older, with the guidance of parents and coaches trained to cultivate the Whole Child—not just the prospective athlete—they can develop into creative, adaptable, healthy young men and women who are confident in their bodies and socially well-adjusted.

When Should My Child Start Organized Sports?

My child is five years old. A lot of the parents around me are busy choosing a sport or sports for their child. But I'm not sure it's the right time for him to start organized sports yet. Will he miss out if I don't start him early enough?

Discussion: Consider your hesitation a blessing, and hold on to it for dear life. What your instincts are telling you is that your child's childhood really matters. Protecting and extending it for as long as possible is one of our biggest responsibilities as parents.

You've heard this often, but it bears repeating: Kids today are overscheduled by their parents in hypercompetitive situations. They are also overstimulated by an onslaught of media messages, which trigger anxiety about their looks, performance, and potential. No wonder their young minds and bodies are overwhelmed. Children need room to breathe, stretch, and grow at a healthy pace. If we shove our kids into an army of minivans and deck them out in uniforms to patrol the fields of hyperorganized sports when they haven't yet had the time to enjoy play's formative stages, we are interfering with their physical and emotional development.

We delve deeper into this in chapter 4, but the timeline goes something like this: Solitary play—the domain of babies and toddlers—gives way to parallel play, in which they experiment playing alone next to others. Then comes the "let's pretend" stage, during which five- to seven-year-olds dress up as knights and princesses and explore the field of their imagination.

If your child is tossed into structured team play too early, his days of imaginative discovery are cut short. He's thrust into an environment much like school, where adults govern and rules and procedures are predetermined and inflexible. At this age he needs more free time to explore and connect with the world on his own terms. He's told what to do enough at school and at home. Some time must be set aside for him to simply play, by himself and with friends, with little outside direction.

As your child reaches the ages of eight, nine, and ten (certainly not five!), he tosses aside his cape and sword and steps across the threshold into what play experts call the "game stage" of play. At this point, he and his friends devise and adapt the games they engage in (like tag, four square, and capture the flag) to satisfy two primary goals: have fun and keep playing for as long as possible.

It's during these self-directed "pretend" and semistructured "game" stages of play that your child develops the all-important emotional intelligence child experts rave about. Working things out with his peers, your son learns impulse control and cooperation. This is when he is called upon to develop and exercise creativity and adaptability, two key skills that unfortunately have little opportunity to flourish in the command and control universe of adult-oriented youth sports. There, coaches, like their teaching counterparts in school, often scrutinize and control every step of the learning process.

Solution: Sit your partner down at the kitchen table when your son is fast asleep. Share your sports parenting goals. Determine if they align. If one of you is pushing for organized sports involvement, be respectful of that point of view, but delve deeper. Explore the roots of this urge to plunge into the petri dish of organized sports now. Start by taking a step back and asking, "Why do we want our child to play organized sports?"

Is it because you hope he will eventually capture an NCAA scholarship? (Fewer than 1 percent of high school athletes do.) Are you convinced that he's the next Tiger Woods or Venus Williams? Do you feel that if you don't get him "on the right track" right now, he'll be at a disadvantage for the rest of his "athletic career"?

If so, consider realigning your goals. He's five. There's plenty of time. For every top athlete who had a golf club or soccer ball thrust into his crib, there's one who took up the sport she now plays with professional prowess when she was twelve years old.

Perhaps you simply want your son to learn teamwork and discipline and how to interact well with other kids. However, you may be introducing him to organized sports before he's physically developed enough to withstand the demands of practice, or mentally prepared to handle the pressure of competing in a socially demanding setting. That may not be in the best interest of your Whole Child. Peer pressure can be powerful, but don't succumb just because some of your friends do. Devise *your* own plan, figure out the appropriate pace for *your* son, and set a course *you* are comfortable with.

True, he may be itching to join in (kids do love those uniforms), but you can provide him with the gift of anticipation. Explain to him that, in a few years, he will get to play on a team, but for now you want him to explore other activities. Let the excitement build. He may hound you at first, but hold steady. Set him up so he can experience the joys of free play with friends (see our suggestions for fun backyard and park play in chapter 6), and when you can, take him on exploratory adventures like long walks or hikes and bike rides with Mom and Dad. Let him play his heart out in the backyard and with friends at the park while you sit by, book in hand, ready to wade in if things get too heated or he wanders too far from view. All the while he will be developing the skills—physical, social, and mental—to excel in organized sports when he's wholly ready to take up the challenge.

Are Travel Teams Essential?

Should my nine-year-old play on an elite team? Many of her friends are doing this, but I worry that it will be too much stress and infringe too much on our family time.

Discussion: Travel teams were designed for high-school-age youths who are ready to specialize in a particular sport and can make complex judgment calls. Our perspective, based on long experience, tells us that children under the age of fourteen should not be subjected to the intensity of travel team competition. They are not ready physically, as has become clear by the rash of wear-and-tear injuries doctors have recently diagnosed in nine- and ten-year-olds (injuries typically incurred formerly by adult athletes).

They aren't ready emotionally, either. The stress of high-level competition can be detrimental to their young, forming minds. It can prompt indiscriminate risk-taking and aggressive behavior or result in low self-esteem. We have to remind ourselves that little kids are sensitive. They take failure very personally. As sports psychologist Richard Ginsburg, author of *Whose Game Is It, Anyway?*, points out, "a child [at Little League age] cannot differentiate their performance with who they are as a person." Coaches and teachers should encourage and praise effort rather than *winning*. The pressure to perform stresses kids out, and when playing is no longer fun, kids quit.

Research has shown that young children who specialize in formal sports early are likely to burn out by their early teens. As Tom Farrey points out in *Game On,* the United States has three times as many registered youth soccer players (3.9 million) as Brazil or France. Studies show that participation levels peak at age nine, however, when most Brazilian kids are just starting organized soccer. As they get older, US kids quit in droves.

Parents who buy into the travel team craze are often looking to give their kids a competitive edge, but joining early by no means guarantees skill development. In fact, it can actually stifle or retard a young athlete's development rather than give him a leg up on the competition. As an athletic trainer who specializes in skill development, Scott notes that most of his clients are the parents of kids who play on travel teams. The reason they pay him and other skills coaches large sums of money to train their kids is because they have realized travel team coaches seldom have the time or make the effort to focus on athletic development or skill training. The kids are often not getting the proper attention and training. Travel team coaches have a greater tendency to be focused on winning games rather than developing players, so parents who sign their kids up with travel teams to give them that "edge" are then compelled to dish out even more money and devote more time to getting their kids trained by one-on-one specialists.

Solution: The good news is that there are alternatives to travel teams and specialists. We are talking about an age group that should be having fun and developing athletic skills during free play with their friends. How do you do that? You can simply take them to the park and let them be. Kids are creative. They will figure it out, whether it's a pickup game, tag, or capture the flag, or you can give them the materials to build an obstacle course or a bike ramp in your backyard. You can also "recruit" like-minded parents (see "A Story of Proactive Parents," which follows), but we've found that they will gravitate toward you, because parents instinctively know what healthy free play is. It's what we loved as kids—the freedom to express ourselves outdoors without adult interference. Our kids will love it too, if we give them the chance and the space.

A Story of Proactive Parents

Here's a group of dads who fundamentally changed their sons' football experience. After two seasons of travel tackle football, the dads noticed that their kids' interest in the sport was fizzling. The boys all played on a regular basis and the team was competitive, so riding the bench and frequent losses were not at fault. What it came down to was this: Practices were held too frequently (four to five days a week), and they were boring. The coaches focused primarily on developing game strategy and were teaching way over the kids' heads. Because the kids did not spend enough time learning fundamental skills, they were prone to injuries.

The dads revolted and created a mini program of their own. The game was seven-on-seven, one-hand touch football, played on a much smaller field. The team size and space limitations guaranteed that each kid got many more chances to throw, catch, and run with the ball than he would have had playing on a full squad. Practices were packed with fun drills and activities that kept the kids active and engaged at all times while developing their skills and athleticism. Teams practiced no more than twice a week and played each other on weekends. Occasional tournaments were arranged with neighboring communities.

The result: These children have become passionate about playing football again. Why not? They are having fun and learning skills that make them better players. Other kids in the community have joined in, including many who had never before considered playing football.

The bottom line: Such alternative setups can work in any sport. From a child's perspective, only three ingredients are required: all-inclusiveness, skill improvement, and fun.

Are There Any Travel Team Alternatives?

How can we create alternatives to elite teams if we're looking for something semistructured?

Discussion: Elite teams have overtaken many townships, claiming the available fields and courts. When games and tournaments are scheduled, community authorities even give teams from other towns access to fields and priority over the majority of local kids, who either did not make or did not want to be on a top-tier team.

Solution: Get together with a group of parents and together approach your recreation department or state park to ask about already existing programs in which your children can participate. Or suggest other activities—healthy, all-inclusive alternatives—like the dads in "A Story of Proactive Parents" did. You may not need full fields or courts if you set up small-space games based on skill development (see chapter 6). If you can get enough parents interested, chances are the local recreation department folks will welcome your ideas (their funding often depends on it).

Can Competitive Sports Affect My Child's Friendships?

I hear stories from other parents about my child struggling in his friendships. Does this have anything to do with the competitive sports he is playing?

Discussion: It may, and it may not. Childhood friendships are complicated and multilayered, but we've found that often one of those layers relates directly to what they are taught in child and youth sports settings. Because of the competitive nature of sports and kids' desire to win, they shift from an emphasis on two-way friendships—that are balanced—to alliances. Let's explain that a bit more. If the emphasis is on winning, on being on top, such competitiveness is not really compartmentalized to the playing field or court. When children have had win, win, win repeatedly drummed into them, such an unbalanced value often spills over into their social lives (see "Why Shouldn't We Want to Win at All Costs?" on page 36).

Kids who play a lot of competitive sports can seek to dominate their friends. They may become bossy; they want to be in control and set all the rules of play. They also seek to set the parameters of their friendships, which can become about dominance, not connection. Coaches often tell kids to "control the game" and maintain "possession of the ball" in soccer or basketball, for example. This may become ingrained in them socially. If you are constantly hammering away at a young child about being possessive, they can bring it back into the home and playground. So it doesn't make much sense to discipline a child who refuses to share his toys with his sister if he is told three times a week, by people he looks up to (his coaches), that he should be more possessive. With all this competitiveness, the magic of friendship is at risk of being lost. True connections with other kids can be replaced by strategic alliances.

Solution: If your child exhibits detrimental, hypercompetitive behavior, take action. It's important to limit the amount of competitive sports your child plays in the earlier years. There will be plenty of time for that later, anyway. The key is to match your child with the right age-appropriate activity (see chapter 4). You can wean him off the sport or sports that affect him negatively by limiting participation in that sport to one season per year. And mix things up a bit; introduce your child to other activities, particularly less outcome-based, score-conscious play. You have to de-emphasize winning. There is a time in a child's life, at age twelve or thirteen, when she can make the distinction between being competitive in a sports setting and developing healthy, agenda-free friendships away from the arena, but before then, kids just don't have the capacity to readily differentiate.

We often put our children in sports programs where winning is paramount, hoping they will learn what they need to know to excel in life, and the message they receive is that winning matters most. Ironically, when kids carry that mind-set onto the court of life, they may end up at a stark disadvantage, hobbled by an inability to relate to other kids and form lasting relationships. The win-at-all-costs mantra they absorb on the field can lead to unhappiness and confusion when they apply it to interrelating with parents (with whom they argue to no end), with siblings (whom they may taunt and constantly try to outshine), with friends (who can get turned off because they don't enjoy being bossed around all the time), and at school (where teachers strive for class harmony, not singular superiority). The bottom line? It's unfair to the child. All this win, win, win they are taught on the field can put them in a no-win predicament in life.

Is My Child Ready to Play a Certain Position?

My twelve-year-old son, Billy, plays on a Little League Baseball travel team. Like most of the kids on the team, he's into the idea of pitching, but he has not taken the mound yet this season. The other night the entire team arrived late for a game. They rushed through a five-minute warm-up, and, as threatening clouds gathered on the horizon, the coach called everyone to the bench and announced that Billy was pitching. He immediately took Billy to the field and asked him to throw some pitches (ten in total), and then pronounced, "You're ready." I was alarmed. Even I knew that was not a proper warm-up for a regular starter, let alone a kid who hadn't pitched once for the entire season. Then the game began. What should I have done?

Discussion: This is certainly a sticky situation, and it happens more often than one would think. In the heat of the moment, coaches (and parents) can lose sight of the big picture. There are four different issues at play here.

From a conditioning perspective, no child, starting pitcher or novice, should take the mound without a well-rounded, carefully executed twenty- to thirty-minute warm-up. Without it they are just not ready to throw effectively.

The medical experts we consulted also balked when we described this scenario. Dr. Neil A. Roth, an orthopedic surgeon and sports medicine specialist who has worked with the Los Angeles Lakers and the New York Yankees, and treated young athletes since 1998, pulls no punches. "I would never let this kid go on the mound. At all. He's at prime risk for injuries at multiple levels."

And what about the boy's emotional health? As Dr. Roth— who has coached his two young sons' baseball teams—stresses, "more than anything else, if this boy doesn't get injured physically, he's being set up for failure. Going in cold, without the proper preparation, without working on the mechanics of pitching and building up his confidence on the mound over the course of the entire season—he will most likely do poorly and never want to pitch again."

Last, but not least, on a personal level this is a tough situation for both father and son. Dad knows how excited Billy is to finally get a chance to pitch, and he doesn't want to embarrass Billy in front of his teammates or confront the coach publicly. He wants be seen as cooperative, as doing what's best for the team.

Solution: As parents, we have to bite the bullet in such situations and speak up. Don't call the coach out in public, however; that will embarrass and annoy him. Remember, he's in a pressured situation, looking for a solution to a problem. He needs a pitcher, fast. It's been a long season, and he's had to use his regular starters a lot in the past few weeks. He's responsible for the entire team and is looking for a quick fix. The clouds are rolling in, everyone's traveled all this way, and the game has already been compromised by the team's tardiness.

Be sensitive to your son's plight, too. Explain what can happen if he pitches without the proper preparation. Promise him you will work with him in the backyard or at the park, and that you'll speak to the coach and get him another shot at taking the mound when he's developed the proper mechanics and built up enough body strength and stamina. He may be angry with you at first. That's understandable. He's disappointed. He has a subjective perspective and is being denied something he wants. As hard as it is, you are responsible for the *whole child,* whose long-term health and happiness trump short-term disappointments. When his anger has subsided or the moment is right, tell him a story of disappointment from your own sports biography. The key is to show him empathy without caving in to his short-term expectations.

The bottom line: Your child's physical and emotional health are at risk. Your parental responsibility is clear. Take the coach aside and tell him, quietly but firmly, "Tonight's not Billy's night, coach. My boy needs more time to work on this." The coach will understand and figure out something else. If he puts up a fight and questions your commitment to the team, he probably isn't the right coach for your son.

You are not being unreasonable at all. For starters, as we just mentioned, if Billy—with little to no training—does poorly at such an impressionable age, his confidence can be destroyed. He may never want to go out there again. With so many kids quitting sports at such an early age, the last thing we all want is to lose him.

The risk of injury is real: "He could suffer from an irritation or inflammation of any of the muscles or tendons of his elbow," says Dr. Roth. "He could also develop Little Leaguer's elbow or shoulder, which are very significant injuries. They are essentially stress fractures. He could also injure anything in his lower body."

Another thing to consider: Some of these twelve-year-old batters can really rip the ball. With so little experience on the pitcher's mound, does Billy know how to get into the proper fielding stance after he throws the ball? Or is he a sitting duck forty-two feet from the plate, in danger of being shelled? Even if he doesn't get injured, he's putting other kids at risk because he doesn't yet have enough control over his pitches and can hit batters inadvertently.

A kid needs to practice and get comfortable on the mound in order to master the mechanics of pitching. Parents and coaches should pay special attention to velocity, making sure the child does not overthrow. It's not just his upper extremity; it's his entire body that has to move toward the plate, and the power must be generated from his lower body. Some athletic kids can pitch effectively right off the bat, but most can't. Either way, their technique needs to be developed at practice before they ever take the mound.

You can work with your child on all of this at home first. Read up or consult an experienced coach about proper warm-up routines. The warm-up before a game is pivotal. Kids should toss the ball lightly, first at varying distances (multiple repetitions), before shifting to wind-up warm-ups for the game. Such preparations should take twenty to thirty minutes, not five. Think about it. Professionals go through hour-and-a-half-long warm-ups before every game. Perhaps it's time for the policy folk at Little League headquarters to mandate properly timed and executed warm-ups for all players—not to mention institutionalized training for volunteer coaches who oversee such warm-ups. At the very least, parents should be prepared to step in when such circumstances arise, in any sport. Your child deserves better. Insist on it.

Too Much Pressure, Too Soon

Picture a Little League tournament on a bright sunny Saturday afternoon in upstate New York. Over one hundred teams of boisterous eleven- and twelve-year-old boys have gathered to compete. A type-A coach, much too personally invested in the success of his players, leans against the chain-link fence as one of his boys heads from the batter's box to the plate. "Come on, Aaron! Be somebody!" The little boy glances back at his coach nervously. Then he taps his bat on the plate and cocks his shoulder, trying his best to look good. Before a single pitch is thrown, that coach mindlessly yells out three more times, "Be somebody!" Then, just as the pitcher coils back to hurl the ball at the plate, the coach punctuates his pep talk with six corrosive words: "Are you going to be somebody?"

How does an eleven-year-old digest that kind of pressure? The question may seem relatively harmless to some. Perhaps the coach means to convey that the team is behind Aaron, and the coach just wants him to do his best. But those six words are undermining at best—a perfect setup for abject failure. Essentially, the message little Aaron receives, as he prepares to take his first swing in front of all his teammates, the team parents, and a multitude of strangers—a setting ripe with potential disappointment, and worse, public humiliation—is this: Listen, kid. If you don't get a hit, you are a loser, down to your very core. Worthless. A nobody. A failure. A letdown to all of us who have invested our time in you. Get a hit, man, and you'll be somebody. Otherwise you are nothing.

What many coaches and, sadly, some parents don't seem to get is that young kids are not readily able to distinguish between the failure to succeed and their own self-worth. So when a child plays, it's important to shy away from pressure-stoking comments like the one just described. Instead, we ought to stress repeatedly that the outcome is not the essential part of an experience, just one component.

We all say things without thinking, but all that tongue wagging has consequences. Young kids do not "harden" or "toughen up" because they've been subjected to repeated brow-beating; they simply wither and may well shut down. What's at risk of being destroyed in such moments, little by little, is a critical kernel of self-confidence, which will best grow with the proper nurturing and nutrients.

That's not to say that you should be a fake around your kids—falsely upbeat and bubbly in the face of their failures. But, really, think about it. They know when they've erred. A parent pointing this out to them does no one any good. Little or nothing is gained, and a lot is risked. If they bring up their failure, discuss it with them and help give them context: "This is just one of thousands of games you'll play, Jimmy. It was a tough loss, sure. But let's focus on something we can control. What do you think went wrong? Do you want to practice that play with me this weekend?"

What Can I Do When Expectations Compromise Relationships?

My husband, Bob, and our son Brad are soccer fanatics. Bob's coached Brad for years, but I'm worried he pushes Brad too hard. Brad plays on his high school team and two travel teams now. He seems worn out. I want to step in and tell my husband that Brad needs time away from soccer, but they are so intense about it, and it's really their main way of connecting. What do I do? If I insist that my husband pull back, I worry that their relationship will be compromised.

Discussion: You are right to be worried. Their passion for soccer may be the foundation of their relationship right now, but let's separate today from the past and the future. In our experience, nine out of ten times a bond built around involvement in a sport was a lot stronger a few years back, when father and son were out in the park kicking a ball around and having a whole lot of fun. That's certainly when things were a lot healthier, long before pushiness and pressure became the norm.

All relationships shift over time, but the big danger here is that your husband is putting all of his relationship eggs in one basket. Given what we know about the percentage of kids who burn out and quit in their early teens (about 70 percent), the relationship could be at risk. The harder your husband pushes, the more likely your son will eventually quit. If your son does become fed up and abandon the sport, that single bridge between father and son may well collapse. No farmer grows the same crop year after year, because his soil would stop yielding a healthy harvest. If your husband cultivates his relationship with your son through a single sport, and that activity is spoiled by performance pressure, they are in danger of losing something really precious—something much more important than the sport itself.

Solution: There are two ways out of this precarious situation. First of all, Dad has to get the message to stop pushing so hard. It's great that father and son have bonded so well. Sports can be pivotal to developing strong parent-child relationships. But the onus is on the parent to evolve. It's time for him to dial back the pressure a bit.

Talking about this with your husband may not be easy, but it's truly necessary. If you approach him with an accusatory tone and tell him to back off—in the one area where he connects so fervently with his boy—you are likely to hurt and even infuriate him. That will do no one any good.

It's best to start with affirmation and genuinely compliment him on his dedication to his son. Tell him how thrilled you are that he's spent so much time and energy sharing his passion for soccer and that you want their connection to grow even stronger. For example, you can say, "I'm with you, and I want this to be a key part of our son's life and your relationship with him. I relish all the great moments you and Brad have shared as a result."

Then you can voice your concern that the focus has turned away from Brad and his well-being. Tell him that you are worried that Brad may be under too much pressure, and that you've learned that when kids are pushed too hard, the likelihood they'll quit is high—really off the charts.

Next, suggest that he diversify, that he use the sport as a pillar around which he and his son can do other things. Stop for ice cream or pizza after practice instead of driving straight home. In other words, build a social component around the main activity. Don't just focus on soccer. If Dad is driving Brad to training three nights a week, do something not directly related to soccer on two of those nights. The key is to introduce another relationship connection point.

Once in a while it's good to switch things up altogether. Take a Saturday off from soccer and go hiking or fishing. Shared passion for a sport can be an incredible source of relationship-building, but it has to be cultivated in moderation. Because when you drill down to the core, the priority isn't the sport or your child's performance, it's your bond with him. That's what matters most. That's what will last a lifetime.

What Do I Do if My Child Hates Practice?

Lately my child stops me at the door and asks, "Do I have to go to basketball practice today?" When I ask why, she says, "It's not fun." But in our driveway she'll play pickup for hours. Should I be worried?

Discussion: This is a classic warning sign that your kid may be close to quitting organized sports. Over seventy percent do so by the age of thirteen. In your backyard, your child remains engaged because she is creating her own experience. That's great. Keep her out there playing with friends, making up games, and devising and revising rules. But her involvement in organized sports can also be beneficial as she gets older and her desire to socialize grows.

There are no easy answers here. When you think about your kid quitting sports so early, various scenarios flood into your mind. What if she becomes bored or depressed at home? Will she have trouble making friends? You don't want her to become passive, watch too much TV, or gain weight, either. Then there's risk-taking behavior, a worry for every parent. If she leads an inactive life and has too much time on her hands, anything can happen, right? If she stops playing sports now, will she ever get the chance to excel and play at the high school level and perhaps even in college? Let's take a deep breath and not get ahead of ourselves, and instead just tackle the issue at hand.

Solution: Before you try to convince your kid to stay with the sport she's playing, stop and think about it. Maybe she is right. Maybe she needs to spend a bit more time participating in free and semistructured play. Arrange more backyard time for her. You can also take her down to a skate park if you have one nearby, or to the climbing wall at the local gym, if one is available. The important thing is to give her a chance to try out a range of activities.

Listen to her carefully. We often push our kids when they put up resistance at the doorway. We say, "Get your stuff. We're going. You've made a commitment to your team." But if your daughter is on the younger side (eleven or under), she may simply be overwhelmed by the experience of playing on a team or dislike the game or coach. She may just need more downtime, especially if she's involved in various other weekly activities, such as music or dance. If that's the case, it may be best to pull back and reintroduce team sports down the line.

If she's eleven or twelve and not overbooked, more exploration is in order. Ask her if there is anything she likes about practice. How about the sport? Every child is different, but she is now at an age when you can start asking her, "What are your goals?" She can begin to formulate her approach to life and, with your stewardship, of course, test out and choose her own interests.

Your conversation with her can center on two basic principles: (1) is what she is doing helping or hindering her goals, and (2) is there something you can do to help her achieve her goals? Having a conversation like this is better than trying to convince or force your child to do what you think is right for her. That's about your goals, not hers. So when you are at the door and she is complaining about practice, you can ask point-blank, "What do you want to do with this sport?" She may say, "I don't know. My friends are trying out for travel." Your conversation might continue something like this:

"Do you want to be on a travel team?"

"Yeah."

"Really?"

"Yeah."

"Well, do you think not going to practice is going to get you onto the travel team?"

If she responds by saying, "No. I don't want to be on the travel team. I just want to have fun," you can make the distinction clear to her. "Okay, then, that's the rec league you are in. You only have one practice a week. But if you don't go to it, then are you really participating?"

By having an open discussion with your daughter, you are calibrating what she really wants to do, which she may be trying to figure out herself on the fly. Because at this age (twelve, thirteen, and fourteen), she is just developing her own ideas. Listen to her carefully. Her friends, by this age, are as big an influence on her as you are, but if you listen to her, she will always come back to you and weigh your input appropriately. She may well feel heard and respected, and that can make all the difference in your relationship and her involvement in what she most wants to do. Then you can make a final decision. Because at this stage, of course, the decision is ultimately yours, but at least she will feel that she has some ownership over her destiny.

Possible Consequences of Quitting Sports

None of us want our children to be quitters. We all want them to socialize with their peers, be a part of a team, and get good exercise. If your child does stop playing sports, even temporarily, make sure he has a plan B that is productive. Otherwise he may:

- Lose valuable time with friends
- Become bored, isolated, or even depressed
- Passively watch too much TV and screens in general
- Gain weight due to inactivity
- Increase the tendency to fall into high risk taking (for example, alcohol and drug use)
- Pass up a chance to play varsity level or college level sports

Ask Yourself Why Your Child Wants to Quit (Then Ask Your Child, Too)

If your child shows signs of wanting to quit his or her sport, think about what could be causing those feelings. Take it seriously. What is motivating this decision? Is it reasonable? Generally, kids quit for one or more of the following reasons:

- They "hate" the coach or their teammates.
- They no longer enjoy playing the sport or practice is not dynamic enough.
- They realize they cannot compete with their peers (they "ride" the bench).
- They discover a passion for a new sport.

- They simply want to try something different.
- They are exhausted or burned out (physically or psychologically).
- They are simply overwhelmed by the number of activities they are involved in and may need more downtime.

Faking Injuries: A Doctor's Story

While the quantity and severity of youth sports injuries in this country is shocking, even more discouraging is the fact that doctors are encountering kids who fake injuries in a desperate plea to escape pressure exerted by overbearing parents. "It happens quite often," says Dr. Roth. "Parents just ride these kids hard to play and perform. They'll come in faking an elbow or knee injury. Their X-rays are normal. Their MRIs are normal. There's no swelling. But everything hurts. You barely touch them, and they seize up in pain.

"I had one eight-year-old child come in here bellowing about severe knee pain. His father had been an elite NCAA Division I basketball player. The child himself was a terrific athlete. But the dad was putting a ton of pressure on the little guy. I asked to see the routine he had his kid going through each day. He had him doing sprints, leg lifts, and all kinds of other track and conditioning exercises. It clearly drove the boy a little nuts."

The mom? She was beside herself. But family power dynamics were at play here. "A lot of times the mothers will say, 'We are not playing this anymore,'" says Dr. Roth. "'Enough. It's not worth it.' But then they have to go home and contend with Dad. And God knows what he's saying to them when they get there. There can be plenty going on."

In such situations Dr. Roth chooses his words wisely: "Look. I'm not sure there's much here," he'll say. "Let's try to treat your son a little bit, but there might be other things going on." He then takes each parent aside and asks what's going on at home. "Does your son really want to play this sport?" he'll ask. "And based on what I hear, I'll say, 'Look. Maybe give him a break. Don't make him play for a while and see if he bounces back and wants to get at it again at some point.'"

In the case of the little hoopster, Dr. Roth counseled moderation. "His dad was about to send him off to camp to train more." Roth recommended that he take some time off away from basketball, do some physical therapy, and cross-train a little bit. Instead of playing basketball, he could do some unrelated stretching and strengthening, bike riding, or any other activity that worked his muscles in a different way. That would enable him to become more adaptive and flexible. "All that sport-specific training was getting to him," says Roth. "That, and the pressure from his dad, were wearing him down."

Mom's reaction to the doctor's prescription? She cried and hugged and kissed Dr. Roth. "Thank you so much for giving him a break from this," she said.

• • •

In the last two chapters we have shared stories about well-meaning parents who have, quite unintentionally, negatively affected their children's experiences in youth sports. Sometimes it's been due to a lack of awareness of the pivotal role our past plays in determining how we shape our hopes and expectations for our kids. In other cases it's been because we have an overwhelming urge to provide them with the best tools possible to build a roadway to success. The best thing we can do for our novice athletes is to step back a bit, withdraw to the sidelines, and observe. Let them know that we are right there, ready to swoop in if they are in need of our care and attention, but not hovering, not casting a long shadow of judgment over their newfound freedom. In the next chapter we will make the case for more free, unstructured play and games, which have benefits that reach far into adulthood. Perhaps, as we learn to draw back a bit, some of the playfulness and joy we witness will rub off on us as well.

CHAPTER 4

The Power of Play

On a scorching August afternoon, University of North Carolina women's lacrosse coach Jenny Levy tours Chapel Hill's verdant college campus with a top recruit she hopes to woo into her elite program. Levy and her prospect happen upon a group of Levy's varsity team players, running through drills at an unofficial preseason practice.

You'd think the top tier NCAA Division I coach would be elated. Her girls are out there, pounding the grass in what feels like an almost scripted display of off-season initiative. But Levy has mixed feelings. "I'm glad they're out there training, but I'd be much more excited if they had flipped their goals upside down or placed them back-to-back to mix things up a bit," she says. "They are kind of like overbred dogs, mimicking the drills we run twice a week in practice. They do what they know. What's safe. I'd much rather see them trying something totally outrageous and different. I want them to get creative on that field."

It's Levy's biggest challenge: to force her hypertrained, overtaught players to think on their feet, to play creatively. She spends hours designing and redesigning her practices to address this deficiency head-on. "Unless they had an amazingly creative youth sports coach—and most haven't—kids simply aren't wired to think creatively in game situations," she says. "Starting at a very young age, there's always been an adult telling them what to do, where to stand, when to move. They may be talented, or physically fit, but if I want them to be creative, I have to retrain them."

To combat this dearth of creativity and adaptability, Levy constantly changes the rules and parameters of drills and games. She jostles her players out of their comfort zones and forces them to adapt instantaneously to revised circumstances. For example: On a traditional lacrosse field, two six-by-six-foot goals face each other at opposite ends of a 100-yard field. "So I'll use four goals instead of two and place them all over the field rather than directly opposite each other," says Levy. "Suddenly players can score in different ways. When you change the dynamics, you force them to think differently, to adapt. To devise ways to adjust. Change the space. Change the equipment. Change the rules. Then do it again. We'll alter the dimensions of the field, or the location of the goals. We might use tennis balls instead of lacrosse balls. The key is to switch things up on them so that they always feel a little bit uncomfortable and have to figure things out for themselves."

Levy is not the only educator grappling with recruits who lack creativity and adaptability. This is a cross disciplinary concern. Kevin K. Parker, professor of bioengineering and applied physics at Harvard, says it takes him years to deprogram students who have been taught in conventional classrooms. Only then can they become innovative, creative thinkers in a laboratory setting. "One of the biggest challenges I have is taking [those] straight-A students and pulling them outside the box. They are raised in a classroom making straight A's. You ask them into a lab, and you are asking them to tear apart everything they know, everything about their safe zone."

At Stanford University, Dr. Carol Dweck encounters students who want to look smart rather than get smarter. In her book *Mindset,* she sets out a thoroughly researched case of how overpraise, overtraining, and overstructuring can produce young people who do not live up to their potential. "In fact, every word and action sends a message," she says. "It tells children—or students or athletes—how to think about themselves. It can be a fixed mindset message that says: 'You have permanent traits and I'm judging them.' Or it can be a growth mindset message that says: 'You are a developing person and I am interested in your development.'"

Too often our child-athletes have been similarly overprogrammed and overtrained, starting at too early an age. Whole Child Sports wants to change that. We recommend a timeline that respects and promotes the free play and game play stages of a child's personal and athletic development, pivotal phases in which children can learn and cultivate attributes essential to their future success on the field and beyond.

We are not way out on a limb here. There is nothing radical or granola / tie-dye about what we suggest. Child development experts—or play theorists—have touted the benefits of informal sport and game play since the early 1960s. Think sandlot baseball in middle America or pickup pond hockey in colder climes; beach and alleyway soccer in the favelas of Brazil, and baseball played with bottle cap "balls" and broomstick "bats" in the backwater towns of the Dominican Republic. These settings are the contextual equivalent of superlabs, where über-athletes like Satchel Page, Wayne Gretzky, Pelé, and Vladimir Guerrero developed and honed the skill sets and creative flair that catapulted them to superstardom. "The best athletes in the world have had formal training at some stage, but what distinguishes them from the rest is what they did as kids when they were alone or with friends, just messing around," says Levy. "Like backyard ball, where they worked on skills naturally. Not surrounded by cones and barking adults."

Sadly, such natural developmental petri dishes are a rarity today. Probably like you, back when we were growing up, the opportunities for free play and games were plentiful. All you had to do was step out your back door, rustle up some friends, and get on with it. We'd lose ourselves for hours on end, often returning only as darkness fell or the call to supper rang out. For many those days are gone. Perhaps Dr. Neil Roth—youth sports medicine specialist and father of two—characterizes it best: "In my neighborhood you went into the street and found friends who were out and did whatever. Climb trees. Play ball. There is none of that going on in my community today. I can count on one hand the number of times I've seen kids in our neighborhood go out and just have completely unorganized, unstructured play time."

Where did all the children go? And why? Take a drive through urban America or suburbia, and you can bear witness to the nearly empty parks and derelict outdoor facilities. There is little going on out there that isn't organized and run by adults. As Mike Lanza, author of *Playborhood: Turn Your Neighborhood into a Place for Play*, points out, "Kids are typically doing one of two things these days. They are either sitting in front of screens too much—up to eight hours a day on average. Or they are being chauffeured around to highly structured, adult-led activities."

One reason why is that parents are struggling to overcome their fears. Child safety is foremost in our minds, and mostly with good reason. Many neighborhoods are unsafe. But even in secure areas, few kids are permitted to wander, and if a kid does walk around the neighborhood, he is unlikely to find anyone else to play with anyway. The very fact that a Mike Lanza exists—someone who has created a micromilieu in which his kids and all the children in his immediate neighborhood can gather the way we all did every day as kids—is emblematic of how radically things have changed, and most would agree this change has not been for the best. It's almost unbelievable that a dad who wanted his kids to experience self-directed fun could be such an outlier.

What does it say about our society that a father was compelled to write a book that could serve as a blueprint for parents in neighborhoods across the country who want to create conditions in which kids can have healthy fun as we did naturally twenty or thirty years ago? Lanza is an inspiration to us all, and a growing number of parents feel that he's absolutely right. We need to bring back free play, in a big way. It's critical to our children's individual and collective well-being. Unstructured and semistructured play, whether sports based or not, are essential pathways through which our kids achieve social, emotional, and cognitive development. Games like tag, four-square, and capture the flag, to name just a few, are much more than simple childhood activities. These are pivotal experiences in childhood development. Socially, we are talking about improvements in your child's problem-solving, flexibility, and conflict-management skills. Emotionally, the benefits include "self-concept," or the strengthening of self-image, as well as moral reasoning and the ability to take perspective (see the bigger picture in a situation). Cognitively, kids develop creativity and spatial reasoning through such activities.

So why are we, as a society, so hell-bent on structuring so many of our children's waking nonschool hours (if we have the time and can afford to)? Much of the anxiety that drives society's unwavering preoccupation with results (winning at all costs) in youth sports springs from a perfectly healthy and natural desire to see our children succeed in sports and in life. We hustle and bustle about, trying to create perfect—or near perfect—conditions that can help catapult our children into the promised land: a good college, an invigorating career, monetary success, lifelong comfort. Even before their child turns five or six, some parents max out their credit cards, placing Sarah on soccer teams, in music camps, in art programs, and everything else they can rationalize as the must-have footholds of her developmental climb to the rarified heights of superachievement.

We tend to do all these things because we want to provide our kids with the best possible tool kit for accomplishment, a grab bag of skill sets they can utilize to get ahead. Any advantage, of any kind, will do. The stark reality is that our kids have to be prepared to reinvent themselves often, and on the fly, to jump-start entrepreneurial ventures when jobs with established companies are scarce. Because, let's face it, it's not getting any easier out there. The middle class is shrinking; the job market is ever more fickle. Corporations have long since jettisoned their paternalistic ways. Generous medical, dental, and pension plans are nostalgic memories, except in the corner offices of the tallest edifices.

Back in 2006, the United States Department of Labor reported that your son or daughter would likely remain at a particular job—on average—for two to three years, tops, and that figure continues to shrink. As Noel Wagner, director of talent acquisition at the Achilles Group, wrote in 2012, "People used to stay with their companies until retirement." Ten years ago, she adds, it was typical to see people staying in their jobs for five to ten years. Then the average tenure dropped to three years. "Now we're seeing that 18 months is normal."

The bottom line: Your child is going to have to be quick on his feet and know how to adapt. That's why we spend so much family time and resources building a platform of opportunities for our children, right? Team sports, lessons, extra tutorials.

What's counterintuitive about all this, and quite shocking, is that this investment may be misplaced or misguided. Or at the very least, ill-timed. As Carol Dweck acknowledges, "No parent thinks, 'I wonder what I can do today to undermine my children, subvert their effort, turn them off learning, and limit their achievement.' Of course not. They think, 'I would do anything, give anything, to make my children successful.' Yet many of the things parents do boomerang. Their helpful judgments, their lessons, their motivating techniques often send the wrong message."

Perhaps we should hit the pause button and ask ourselves, what is the return on investment (ROI) here? Why—if we want our kids to get ahead, and stay ahead—do Jenny Levy,

Professor Parker, and Dr. Dreck have to unteach much of what we've spent good money on to have programmed into our kids' brains from the start? Could we be approaching education from the wrong angle? Is this platform of opportunities we work so hard to set up built on shaky foundations?

One of the most dynamic buzzwords in the halls of corporate America these days is *executive function*. Many of the top companies want their new hires to score high on the EF scale. Yet executive functioning is not a skill set one develops in the myriad hyperorganized, adult-led extracurricular activities we funnel our children into for so many hours after school. Executive functioning is developed most effectively in the context of imaginative, unstructured free play. Erika Christakis, MEd, MPH, an early childhood teacher and former preschool director, and her husband, Nicholas Christakis, MD, PhD, a professor of medicine and sociology at Harvard University, have witnessed up close the executive functioning deficiency of today's college students while serving as masters of Pforzheimer House, a Harvard undergraduate residential house. In a December 2010 CNN.com article they wrote, "Every day where we work, we see our young students struggling with the transition from home to school. They're all wonderful kids, but some can't share easily or listen in a group. Some have impulse control problems and have trouble keeping their hands to themselves; others don't always see that actions have consequences; a few suffer terribly from separation anxiety. We're not talking about preschool children. These are Harvard undergraduates whom we teach and advise. They all know how to work, but some of them haven't learned how to play." Their observations are buttressed by a 2006 study from the American Academy of Pediatrics that points out that free and unstructured play "is healthy and—in fact—essential for helping children reach important social, emotional, and cognitive developmental milestones as well as helping them manage stress and become resilient."

Early childhood teachers, developmental psychologists, and neuroscientists have been saying this for decades, but it bears repeating: "One of the best predictors of school success is the

---

Playborhood author Mike Lanza turned the front and backyards of his Menlo Park, California, home into an oasis for play. The ideology that motivated his efforts to transform his neighborhood is one we can all aspire to.

THE PLAYBORHOOD MANIFESTO

I want my kids to play outside with other neighborhood kids every day.

I want them to create their own games and rules.

I want them to play big, complex games with large groups of kids, and simpler games one-on-one with a best friend.

I want them to decide for themselves what to play, where, and with whom.

I want them to settle their own disputes with their friends.

I want them to create their own private clubs with secret rules.

I want them to make lasting physical artifacts that show the world that this is their place.

I want them to laugh and run and think.

Inspired by Lanza's example, parents from around the country have taken up the torch. "The key is to create a sense of community among parents and kids," says Lanza. "When people get to know each other better, they look out for each other's kids, and everyone feels safer. And that's a stepping stone to kids playing together more and becoming more independent themselves."

---

ability to control impulses," Team Christakis writes. "Children who can control their impulse to be the center of the universe, and—relatedly—who can assume the perspective of another person, are better equipped to learn." That's why free play is so important. It's a world in which children witness and learn about each other's emotions and develop collaborative skills. When children play imaginatively, they develop empathy and self-regulatory abilities.

In this chapter we explore the importance of play and games, and take a look at how sports and athletic development intersect with free play and can be enhanced by a healthy dose of unstructured play, before and during a child's active participation in organized sports.

Are Organized Sports Eroding My Child's Imagination?

Before he began playing organized sports, my seven-year-old had a really rich imagination. He seemed to be able to make sense of the world by working things out through play. He isn't doing that much these days. I know I've got a lot to worry about as a mom. Should I add this to my list?

Discussion: You've hit on a really important issue here, and you're right to be worried. Youth sports are hyperorganized and adult oriented. Structured, organized sports are taught predominately through command instruction: The coach tells you what to do, how, and when. Command instruction, unfortunately, limits creativity. It's great for army platoons, but not so good for kids.

Pretty much all the experts will tell you that this is an age and stage when it's best for your child to be engaged in self-structured play (by which we mean activities that he creates for himself) and games (like tag, capture the flag, and catch) that have very flexible parameters. Even scrimmaging, which some folks would argue is semistructured free play, can force children to play under traditional rules that box them in. They are often reenactments of adult-oriented rules and games, and therefore do little to promote creativity, unless the kids are in charge and feel free to adjust the rules and negotiate conflicts with playmates.

Creativity is a process that involves your child's imagination, exploration, and self-discovery, and your hunch that it's good for your kid is spot-on. As Kim writes in *Simplicity Parenting*:

> In free play, children have to actively problem solve and to take one another's feelings into account if the play is going to be successful. Success in free play simply means the game continues, and continues to be fun. "What should I do if this is, like, the coolest game ever, but Alex doesn't want to crash the cars? It's no fun without him, and plus, he'd take the red car with him if he goes." When everyone has a stake in the play, feelings must be taken into account. In sport, the social problem solving is largely extrinsic, facilitated by coaches, referees, or parents. During a child's formative stages, between five and twelve, having the freedom to develop, create, and innovate is critical.

This issue is by no means limited to younger children. The way sports are taught at all levels, right up through high school, often inhibits athletic creativity and problem solving—as UNC coach Jenny Levy has seen in the freshman players she trains year after year—rather than fostering them.

You can teach kids the fundamentals, but then you have to leave them alone. The great moves will come to them when they are on their own: that amazing drag-back move with a quick stutter step and change of direction that allows them to blast past defenders, or that combination hesitation-shoulder fake just before they switch hands and drive to the basket.

When left alone or horsing around with their friends in the backyard or park, kids get creative. That's when they develop the flair that we are mesmerized by in elite athletes. It's a crucial stage of athletic growth. We have to find ways to free kids to develop their own unique sporting flair, which helps them sharpen their "competitive edge." It's something unique to them, which they develop on their own. It's not something they can be coached to do. It isn't "trained into" them. It springs from their passion for play.

Solution: There are a number of things you can do to revive your child's imagination. You can simply take him out of organized sports for a while and give him time to rediscover childhood play and games. You can put him back in when he's a bit older. It's important to remember that we are looking at the Whole Child, not just the budding athlete. And it's not just his imagination and creativity that are at stake here. In our experience, kids who get heavily involved in highly structured organized sports too early are at risk for behavioral problems (see chapter 3).

You may feel that organized sports are important for your child socially. In that case, try reducing the amount of time he spends in this highly structured environment. Simply dialing back his involvement—perhaps to one practice and one game per week—may help revive his imaginative play. One thing is certain: Coaches who push for multiple weekly practices for kids in this age group do not necessarily have your child's best interest at heart. Pushing kids and overtraining them at this age is likely to dampen their enthusiasm for sports in later years. It may also increase the likelihood that they are sidelined with wear-and-tear injuries.

The best thing you can do for your child at this age— whether you take him out of organized sports for a while or keep him lightly engaged—is to roll up your sleeves and get involved yourself (see chapter 6). Engage with him in unscripted backyard or park play and activities. Just regular kids' stuff. Add a few of his friends to the mix. Make it fun, but keep it informal. He will thrive in such self-structured and semistructured environments. Your child's sports play should be put in context.

One thing to bear in mind: Free play can come at a bit of a cost. You have to be willing to put up with play that seems a bit chaotic. In order to provide some boundaries, you'll need to make the kids understand that tearing through the house in bunches and knocking things over is for outside. When a cluster of kids is crashing through your backyard or basement, your perfectly organized universe will invariably be affected, but it should not be turned on its head. Your home space can be open to the creative messiness that play brings, but it also needs to be respected.

Finally, kids need to understand that in your house the game ends when they pack up the play equipment and put the house back in some order. Maybe it's not put back perfectly, but good effort needs to be made. If kids walk away from their creative debris, leaving "guess who" to tidy up, they miss an opportunity to learn that play is a process. Like anything else, it has a beginning and an end. It was great that they were there at the beginning of the game, and yes, they should also be there at the end, helping to put away their toys and equipment. Out of chaos, creativity springs forth, and that's the ultimate goal, but hosting a free-play zone does not mean you should become a one-person cleaning crew. Children and neighborhood friends can be taught to deal with the collateral damage of their unstructured fun. They can be made personally responsible for cleaning up the play paraphernalia they've left scattered about.

A Team Pulls Together

Tony, a girls' youth soccer coach from Connecticut, contacted Kim for advice on how to manage the social woes that were fracturing his team, the Red Hawks. He'd already had heart-to-hearts with individual players and convened team meetings. "Good teams don't argue," he told his players. "They don't speak to each other the way you girls do. Things have to change." But airing out their issues did little to resolve things. "It's like a whack-a-mole," Coach Tony told Kim. "No matter what I do to deal with one problem, another one pops up. The team is disjointed. Some girls won't pass to each other. There's no harmony. What can I do?"

The facts: These were skilled eleven- and twelve-year-old players who had played organized youth sports since the tender age of five or six. Kim surmised that most of them had missed out significantly on the game-playing stage of play development. "Bring the girls together for ten or fifteen minutes at every practice and set them up with traditional games," Kim suggested. "Try capture the flag first. If your practice gets rained out, find an indoor court and set up some four square matches.

Then back off and let them play without your input." He gave him a copy of the book he wrote called *Games Children Play*, which has a ton of games that have good skill-related activities while building collaboration through fun.

The coach did just that. He introduced a handful of games to his Red Hawks during their twice-a-week soccer practices. The arguments that ensued were pretty intense, but now their disputes were about rules and boundaries, and who got to do what rather than who was a hog or a nasty person—in other words, about the game at hand. They had to resolve them so they could get to play and have fun, which they did. If things came to a standstill, they worked things out so they could keep on playing. The coach was surprised by the result. It was almost like night and day. The Red Hawks became much more like a real team and started hanging out together a lot more.

The bottom line: These girls had missed the game-playing stage of play development because of their intense involvement in youth sports from an early age. When kids skip the games stage, they don't have many opportunities to learn how to negotiate. They tend to default back to shouting at each other instead of figuring out how to resolve things. They don't easily listen to each other and instead get stuck in a cycle of wanting things their way. It's a hard thing to watch.

From a developmental perspective, during the tween stage—between the ages of nine and thirteen—the brain begins to process multiple variables. In other words, a child starts to realize, "I am not just me, but part of something greater. I am a part of a whole."

At this age, kids' brains are hungry for social experiences that can help strike a balance between "I am" and "we are," between the child and her needs, and those of the group of kids she's playing with. The ideal setting for such experiences is not really hyperstructured, adult-directed team sports—in which the child abides by a predetermined structure and the brain is more passive—but self-created, self-directed game play. In active play, she participates in the process of creating a new structure with her friends, takes part in it, and adapts it if it's not working well.

After Coach Tony introduced a variety of semistructured games in his practices, the players' relationships began to heal. The coach and his team parents made sure to set up social conditions that would further unify the team. They brought the girls together for pizza parties, postgame ice cream runs, and even a weekend dinner in one mom's backyard or at the park. And the kids clamored so much to play games that Coach Tony made it a permanent part of their practice routine.

Playing games, learning to talk things out, and adapting rules and parameters to different circumstances helped the girls become more flexible and creative. They came up with a two-tiered scoring system to even out team strength during practices: Players with more experience were encouraged to pass more to their less-skilled teammates, because if these less-skilled players scored, their goals were worth more. This helped improve everyone's level of play. The Red Hawks became more cohesive, passing more effectively and setting up their defense and counterattacks more efficiently. Players were more willing to speak up if a teammate was hogging the ball rather than allowing feelings to fester.

The girls also became more creative in the face of stronger opponents. The strategy they came up with to combat a much bigger, faster team: shrink the size of the playing field by hunkering down in their own half and relying on occasional counterattacks for offense. Though the Red Hawks were not able to beat the bigger team, they reduced their scoring chances to such a degree that the girls lost by just three goals rather than being blown out as had happened at the beginning of the season. More important, the Red Hawks had become smarter players and better teammates—and had a whole lot more fun out there.

Is There Value to Free Play?

My gut tells me that unstructured and semistructured play is an important part of my kid's growing up. The years go by so quickly! But my husband is really into sports and doesn't see the value of free play. Am I wrong? Does free play lead to a better sporting experience? Because I know he would value that.

Discussion: When kids are thrust into hyperorganized, adult-oriented sports too early, an entire stage of their play development risks being lost. What's required to really function well on a team in a sports environment is good communication, an ability to work well with teammates and negotiate and resolve issues, and the flexibility to think outside the box. Such skills are not easily honed in organized youth sports. They are mainly learned earlier, during your child's developmental play stages or—if she already plays on a team a few days a week—whenever she gathers with friends informally to just play games.

As Luis points out, "My three youngest sons love sports and are always clamoring to play soccer or football or basketball. And they often do: at the park, in our cramped basement, even on the sidewalk or in the courtyard of a friend's building. But for the past few years, they've gathered after school in Central Park with schoolmates of varying ages and played a variety of other games, such as manhunt and capture the flag."

These games take time to organize. The kids cluster together and argue as they choose teams and negotiate what's fair and what's not. Sometimes setting up the teams takes five or ten minutes, and some pretty heated arguments develop. If you are standing within earshot, your "adult" impulse is to jump in and take over: "Listen, kids. You have to make this fair. Joey and Sara are the oldest and fastest, so they should be on separate teams . . . " But if you do that, you take the decision making, deal making, and conflict resolution away from the kids themselves. Believe us, we know how hard it is to back off and stay clear, but the long-term benefits outweigh your instant gratification at having sorted things out so the kids can get on with their game. The best thing parents can do is huddle together at a distance, chatting away, alert enough to intercede if someone gets hurt or things get out of hand.

Playing these games together teaches kids indispensable lessons about figuring things out for themselves and adapting to the social circumstances they encounter. Organized sport does not do that nearly so well: You have a referee who blows a whistle and provides judgment. What happens in the games stage of development—when you are playing games like capture the flag, four square, dodgeball, or the many forms of tag and hide-and-seek—is that you are forced to sort out your own teams. You have to take ownership of your disagreements and work through them; otherwise, the game cannot go on.

With this type of semistructured play, the children set the rules, organize the form of the game, and then—because they helped make it up—are invested in its structure. They will want to maintain that structure—and enforce it. If someone deviates from the rules, they can object. All this develops children's problem-solving and negotiation skills. Moreover, it really brings kids together in a socially dynamic context in which they learn not only about negotiation but also about accepting the differences in each other's points of view.

Solution: It's best if kids set up these games on their own, but as a parent, you can certainly jump-start things by finding and introducing some of these games to them. You can sift through books on games at your local library or visit the games section at WholeChildSports.com, but the key is to create the time and space in which they can play such games and then withdraw so they can sort things out for themselves. Hand them the reins and provide them with the physical and mental space to guide themselves.

If your kid already plays on a sports team and is enjoying it, that's fine, but developmentally he should experience more of the games stage. Here's what you can do: Invite the team over for a barbecue after practice. After everyone has fun eating and socializing, set up some games the team can play. You'll be surprised by the result. Connecting with each other through these semistructured games will help unify the team. In addition, individual players will become more socially adept and innovative. They'll have fewer disruptive arguments (though some discord is to be expected, and occasional clashes are a healthy part of a team's social dynamic) and be less likely to ostracize less-talented teammates. This translates into good teamwork and better play.

Why Is My Young Athlete Always Bored?

At home my son Noah used to be able to find stuff to do to keep himself occupied, but since he's been playing a lot of sports he gets bored so easily. Is there any connection? He keeps bugging me all the time and is only interested in things that are really loud and exciting.

Discussion: You've noticed something really interesting. Before your son was introduced into a superstructured sports environment he worked things out for himself, and he can do that again. He's probably become used to depending on outside direction rather than self-created and self-directed activities.

Solution: When Noah is bored, your impulse might be to suggest a lot of activities for him to do, but before you flood your child's mind with options (which he's likely to reject anyway), let him know that it's okay that there's nothing to do. Parents find it hard to back off and let their children grapple with boredom by themselves. We want to step in to arrange or entertain, to fill that void in some way. We often see our children's boredom as a personal parental failure, that we aren't providing our children with the right developmental experiences or stimulation.

The world we live in today is becoming increasingly unstructured. As we mentioned earlier, jobs are not a long-term proposition anymore. Times are much more fluid. Children have to be prepared to adapt to radically changing circumstances as they become young adults and enter a frenetic job market. So while parents believe that by giving their kids so many opportunities—through multiple activities—to develop many skill sets, they are helping them sharpen their competitive edge, they are actually often dulling their children's creative sensibilities. We've found that when left to their own devices, kids develop and strengthen the creativity and adaptability muscles that will prove crucial in later years as they navigate the strenuous adult world of job market uncertainty with confidence and entrepreneurial flair.

When our children are bored, we have not failed them. Boredom is a gift. It's an opportunity. It can be a precursor to creativity. Therefore, when your child makes the accusatory declaration, "Mom, I'm bored!" tell him, "That's okay. You'll think of something to do." Say it in a dull, drowsy voice, so he realizes he's not going to get much mileage out of pressing you to figure out his next move for him. You should be on your guard. He may attempt to trigger your annoyance. What better way to assuage his doldrums than by nagging until he gets a rise out of you? Essentially, you have to become the most boring thing in the room. You have to outbore the boredom.

As lacrosse coach Jenny Levy—mom to three boys—reveals, "Kids who have some activity crammed in for every day of the week where they follow an adult's instructions or game plan are being limited. They are not learning to self-start. When my kids say, 'Mom, I'm bored,' I say, 'Oh, great. Why don't you guys go stare at each other until you figure out something to do?' And inevitably some sort of game or project will break out. They just need some down time to work it out."

Of course, getting kids to think for themselves requires some parental fortitude. "When boredom breaks out in my house, the kids ask, 'Can I go turn on the TV? Or play a video game?'" says Levy. But she holds her ground. She makes it clear that those two escape hatches are not an option. "I think the need to be entertained all the time is a product of this generation. You're on your iPhone, or iPod, or plopped in front of the TV. That's way too much stimulation."

Think of it this way. Being bored is actually being in a quiet place where you can think and observe. It may not feel like a comfortable place to be for a lot of kids, but once they get used to it, they will handle it better. It will become an exhaling moment, a transitional phase, in which they can learn to generate their own ideas. "It's on them to create their own games," says Levy. "Not me, or my husband, or the babysitter."

Again, it's okay that your kid is bored. You don't have to put her in yet another sports club or dance class just to keep her busy and distracted. Downtime can benefit her immensely.

Corporate America has certainly caught on. Progressive companies like Google, Deutsche Telekom, and French IT services behemoth Atos have gone as far as to adopt measures to ensure that their employees unplug from technology. They have made downtime mandatory. They do it because being disconnected from a 24/7 news-work-technology cycle promotes relaxation and freethinking. Less-harried employees—who can reboot mentally by doing less—can then contribute with renewed zest and creativity when they reengage at work. As Jennifer Sabatini Fraone, assistant director of the Boston College Center for Work & Family, explains, "If people are drained and getting burned out, they are not bringing their best selves to work every day. It has a big effect on their creativity, their energy, their productivity, and their ability to innovate."

The same applies to your child. If he's exhausted all the time because his every waking hour is planned out so that he won't feel "listless" and is always "maximizing his time," collecting skills, and "keeping up" with his peers, he will miss out on a very important developmental state: boredom.

The Double Edge of Play

Play is critical to a well-balanced childhood, and in our technological age, when the time and space to play are shrinking dramatically both at school and at home, there is, thankfully, a growing awareness of its role in a child's development. More and more articles and academic papers touting the value of play are being published. This suggests that, on some level, we are becoming more aware that something absolutely essential to humanity is being threatened by our frenetic lifestyles. Perhaps our gut instinct is saying, "No. Free play is a right of childhood."

Austrian philosopher Rudolf Steiner understood the pivotal role play has in human development: "If a child has been able in his play to give up his whole living being to the world around him, he will be able, in the serious tasks of later life, to devote himself with confidence and purpose to the service of the world."

To bring this issue into sharper focus, we've included a table that lists the essential benefits of play compared with the stark developmental costs to kids who are denied the time and space to experience free play. As renowned educator Friedrich Frobel so aptly expressed it, "Play is the highest phase of child development—of human development at this state. It gives therefore joy, freedom, contentment, inner and outer rest, peace with the world. It holds the sources of all that is good." Perhaps a five-year-old boy named David put it best: "Play is when we don't know we are different from each other."

	BENEFITS OF PLAY
1.	Motor skills are developed
2.	Senses are sharpened
3.	Have appropriate expressions of emotions (empathy)
4.	Foster sharing, turn-taking, cooperation, feeling of well-being
5.	Master sequencing. Learn to put things in order, large to small.
6.	Build perspective-taking skills
7.	Delay gratification and impulse control
8.	Grow vocabulary
9.	Develop flexibility
10.	Practice role-taking, working through fears via assuming archetypal roles
11.	Learn to move between stimulation-activity and calm-relaxation
12.	Expand imagination and creativity
13.	Learn to tell a logical story—script producing
14.	Express active empathy, seeking ways to help others who are struggling
15.	Develop humor; be able to laugh at self as well as with others
16.	Build a sense of mastery and competence
17.	Reduce aggressive behavior
18.	Grow a sense of timelessness, expansion
19.	Adapt to unexpected outcomes; able to accept winning or losing
20.	Accept challenges that require a "stretch" of learning and capacity

COST OF PLAYLESSNESS
Impairment, speech issues
Sensory overwhelm issues, mistrust of bodily sensation
Disassociation from actions
Self-centeredness, poor impulse control, feeling uncentered
Disorganized thinking, feelings, and actions
"If you don't agree with me, you're lying"
"I want it all now!" Attention priority issues
Frustration at not being able to express oneself
Fear of change and problems with transitions
A generalized anxiety that builds over time
Stuck in low to moderate vigilance; jumpy, nervous; sleeping and eating problems
Rigid, narrow experience of the world
Feeling adrift, fear of the future
Schadenfreude (delighting in others' pain and misfortune)
Defensive, come-back oriented, sarcastic
Inferiority, feeling victimized
Emotional brittleness, imploding-exploding
Overly self-aware
Victor or victim; driven to win at all costs through fear of losing status
Over-developed, one-sided skills and mistrust of new learning

Do Girls and Boys Play Differently?

I have a boy and a girl. They play so differently. My son is really into rough-and-tumble games—the furniture takes a beating. With my daughter it's all about her dolls and their clothes and relationships. I don't want to support gender stereotypes, but this is just the way it happened. Should I be pushing my daughter to be more assertive and asking my son to tone it down?

Discussion: This question comes up quite often. We know gender differences can be a touchy subject, so let's be clear from the start: Of course girls can play strongly and assertively in sports. We recognize this and want to encourage it. There are clear developmental differences between girls and boys, however, and we do really need to embrace them and yet be careful to not buy into old stereotypes.

When young girls play, they often work things out and find their way through relationships. In general, the cooperative and collaborative centers of their brains become active quite a bit earlier than they do in boys. In young boys' brains, visual and spatial development are at the forefront. They are more movement oriented and seek stimulation through kinetic play. They want to bump up against things and each other, and wrestle and tumble about.

Solution: Understanding these differences may help you put up with a little more "rough and tumble" in your son and help you see why your daughter plays more quietly, either alone or with her playmates. Neither is a negative, so let's not worry too much about pushing boys or girls in a certain direction. They will develop into healthy, involved athletes and adults if they have good play experiences in their younger years, regardless of our efforts. They can be guided, however, and should be, when things go awry.

As Steve Biddulph underscores in *Raising Boys: Why Boys Are Different—and How to Help Them Become Happy and Well-Balanced Men,* it is crucial that boys learn the boundaries of rough play. They need to be taught how to play without hurting others, and when to stop. This helps them develop the self-control that will allow them to navigate sticky situations later on in life. That's why it's so important that we not back off and say, "They're just being boys," but actually step in when things get too rough and ensure that they understand boundaries.

Girls, on the other hand, can remain in a deep imaginative state—such as dressing and undressing their dolls repeatedly in solitary play. That's fine for a while, but we would likely become concerned if the girl developed a habit of strongly refusing to let anyone play with her or even alongside her or touch anything she is playing with. We can also enliven girls' play by helping them develop more complex story lines for their dolls. Once they are engaged and building relationships through collaborative play, things can turn negative if they lose sight of the boundaries of appropriateness.

Whether it's girls being mean or boys getting carried away, children need to be guided back into a more positive mode of play. We take care not to normalize antisocial play through parental inaction. A "boys will be boys" or "girls will be girls" permissive mentality does not serve our children well. When social "rough and tumble" play manifests itself in girls as quiet but mean words or "dagger looks" and cliquish or overcontrolling behavior, the best thing to do is step right in, just as you would with rough boys, and tell your daughter that this behavior is unacceptable.

A strategy we highly recommend is to Disapprove, then Affirm, and then Redirect. You might say, "Hey Jennifer, we don't talk like that in our family." Then build her back up by saying, "You don't always behave like that. You do perfectly well most of the time. Yesterday you played really well with Michelle and had a great time." Then suggest an entirely new game or activity she can play with Michelle, removing them from the context in which the argument erupted.

When girls learn appropriate social boundaries, it has a positive effect on their future play in sports. They will be less prone to cliquish behavior with teammates, which can often become an overwhelming obstacle to team unity in sports. Talk to any girls' youth coach, and she'll tell you that she spends a lot of valuable time dealing with cliques and hurt feelings, which she'd much rather dedicate to teaching skills or running fun drills.

Boys who learn not to push and shove or "get in someone's space" are learning spatial appropriateness. That will help them function more effectively as part of a team and also improve their understanding of the use of space in movement: moving into space, passing into space. Basically, any child who is taught boundaries understands his or her own space, another's space, and empty space, which is critical to moving a ball around effectively in team sports. (See "What if My Kid Is Too Passive" on page 164.)

• • •

We hope we have made the case that play is a powerful and essential element of every child's life journey. In a society that

THE POWER OF PLAY

so often seems to be set at one speed only—overdrive—we, as the stewards of the early stages of our children's development, have an obligation to protect and preserve a place for play, to provide our children with the physical and emotional space to run free, interact, create, mess up, and recreate.

In the next chapter, we bring into sharp focus the cultural permissiveness that fosters trash talk and elitism, and we offer advice on how to reframe the social context in which our children interact, in the hope that such unhealthy behavioral weeds wither and a more nurturing social dynamic can take their place and thrive.

CHAPTER 5

How to Avoid Creating Entitlement Monsters— Bullying, Trash Talk, Elitism, and Other Assorted Sports Ills

One day, as I (Luis) was walking in a city park with my son, we came across a friendly pickup soccer game. Three brothers, ages six to eleven at the time, were playing against three kids they'd just met. It looked like a whole lot of fun, but Anthony, the youngest brother, was in tears. His nine-year-old brother, Mark, was berating him for missing a tackle.

"You suck, Anthony. You're the worst player ever."

"Yeah. You always mess it up for us," Josh, the eldest brother, chimed in.

The game continued for a few more minutes until Anthony wandered off, biting his lower lip in frustration, and Mark and Josh started shoving each other.

"If you could even, like, shoot straight, we woulda scored five more goals, you loser," Mark said to Josh.

I walked over to their mother, who was sitting on a park bench, reading a magazine, and asked her: "What happened? Why have your boys stopped playing? Why are they fighting?"

She looked at me and shrugged her shoulders, exasperated. "They are always like that. They can barely play together now. Mark is really good at sports. He's hypercompetitive. But you know, that's just how boys are, right? They are so into winning they can be downright cruel sometimes."

I nodded. But as I walked away, I wondered why this mother had given up on moderating her nine-year-old's antics. Why had she decided that this kind of behavior is just part of life and must be tolerated? That it's part of a male child's DNA to dominate, berate, and belittle—to be sarcastic, cynical, or hurtful. What does this say about our sports culture? What does it tell us about our behavioral expectations for our kids?

This is not simply something to ruminate about. It's serious stuff. Recently I almost shut down a soccer game I was refereeing because the boys were pushing, shoving, and elbowing each other, rather than playing the ball fairly. It was the only way they knew how to interact on the field. Their average age? Seven.

Do sports have to be this way? We want our kids to become more human as they grow older, not less. We want them to discover their own humanity during social interactions, through activities like sports. They play to have fun, make friends, develop skills, and discover their own creativity, but too often we see children enact and mimic adult-sanctioned or tolerated behavior on the field of play. When the dehumanization of another child is fueled by fierce competitiveness, why do we let it slide? The message our kids take in is that "in order for me to succeed, I need to make that other kid smaller. That's the only way I'll get bigger. Better. Be the best." If a child is competing against other teams, and even his own teammates, must he diminish them in order to enlarge himself?

In his work with children in the refugee camps and war zones of Northern Ireland, southern Africa, and Cambodia, Kim John Payne witnessed up close the disturbing social dynamics that can lead to genocide. Genocide exists when an entire group of people dehumanizes another. It creates a culture in which negative acts against a people are tolerated, excused, and, worst of all, normalized. This is what was happening in the park, on a much smaller scale, when the mother I met inadvertently normalized her son Mark's behavior during the pickup soccer game, by accepting the cultural attitude that "boys will be boys." Is the dehumanization of one brother or player by another the cultural status quo in youth sports in America?

When Kim speaks to middle and high school students about the dynamics of genocide, the students lean forward, fascinated. They want to know what they can do personally to change such an intolerant world. Kim's response? He challenges them to alter their own behavior in school corridors, locker rooms, and recess grounds: "Every time you dis, insult, or bully a schoolmate, you take a small step toward dehumanizing that person," he tells them. "Each time you withhold a put-down, or reframe it—if you've blurted it out without realizing it—you help to create a more tolerant and inclusive culture."

A bullying, put-down culture dehumanizes, therefore every time we withhold a sarcastic comment, each time we abstain from trash talking or check a child's urge to dis a teammate, we take a stand against the type of behavior that, in its most extreme form, can devolve into genocide. Trash talk, bullying, and put-downs feed off a culture that permits the dehumanization of one person or race by another.

This is upsetting behavior for us all. When an entire people treat another people as less than human, unspeakable horrors can result. What, you may ask, is this extreme, horrific image doing in a youth sports parenting book? If you think we are being inappropriate or, at the very least, overly dramatic, pause for a moment and think about the messages conveyed and reinforced daily in the theater of play we call youth sports. Remind yourself of the full-scale brawls that break out at Pop Warner peewee football league games among adults, of high school sports teams mired in legal disputes over abusive hazing rituals, and of the habitual verbal abuse by coaches and teammates, which cause tens of thousands of kids to quit team sports each year.

Whole Child Sports champions the humanity in all children, no matter what they look like or how well or poorly they play. Our intention is to set a standard of behavior that clearly delineates what can be tolerated at practice, at games, and in any other team setting, because we live in a culture that has become somewhat accepting of put-downs that span the spectrum from slightly hurtful to vicious, a world where bullying and elitism are often present, a society where sarcasm and cynicism are a pervasive form of humor and often flourish unchecked. They cannot be allowed to rule the day.

As parents, we cannot let down our guard. We can't just leave it at "boys will be boys," "girls just get that way sometimes," or "hey, that's just the way the world works, dude. Get real." What Kim, Scott, and I have seen repeatedly is that kids can and will change their behavior according to the clearly articulated expectations and values of their parents and coaches. When kids respond to a situation by saying cavalierly, "Everyone does that, Coach. That's just the way the world is," the answer is quite simple: "That's not the way *this* world is. In the world of this basketball team, on this baseball squad, on this football team, that is not allowed. Is the outer world like that? Maybe. Your behavior elsewhere is your behavior. I have no influence over that. But this team is my sphere of influence, and you may not speak or behave like that on this team. You will not get away with it here." Now that's the kind of coach you want for your kids.

Coaches and parents need to confront negative social dynamics each and every time they surface in order to create a safe haven for each member of the team. If we don't follow through, if there are no consequences, our speeches about appropriate behavior ring hollow. Children revert to the conduct to which they have been conditioned, which permeates the world that surrounds them. What we can do? Whole Child Sports strives to carve out a relatively safe, nurturing environment in which children are both challenged and protected.

In this chapter we examine bullying, trash talk, put-downs, team hierarchy, and favoritism within the current toxic youth sports context and provide suggestions and solutions for creating a healthier setting for your child's athletic development.

A Coach, a Player, and Bullying

Principal Andrew Zitoli, of Millis Middle School in Walpole, Massachusetts, has become a beacon of light at his school and across the country. He addresses students, teachers, coaches, and administrators about bullying and has built a model anti-bullying program for his Millis fifth- and six-graders. Early in his three-decade-long career as an educator and coach, Zitoli had an experience that underscores the role adults play in supporting a culture in which bullying takes root and flourishes, and it has fueled his antibullying crusade to this day.

"Back when I was a classroom teacher, I doubled as a high school football coach at one of the most high-powered football teams in the state of Massachusetts," he says. "I taught fifth grade every day and worked as an offensive line coach after school. Line coaches are not finesse guys. They're grouchy, angry types. It's just a whole different mind-set."

A couple of years earlier, I'd had a fifth-grader named John in my class—a really nice kid, the kind who was friends with everybody. He came to me when he was in eighth grade and said, 'Mr. Zitoli, I'm going to go out for football next year.' 'Fantastic,' I answered. 'You are going to learn all about teamwork, leadership, and hard work.'"

Zitoli was proud of the football program. It was old-school and very successful. That summer he saw John at the weeklong preseason summer camp. "We were tough," he says. "Frankly, our goal was to kill the kids for a week." John was a fourteen-year-old freshman and Coach Zitoli worked with the varsity squad, so the two did not interact much. But one day, near the end of a grueling afternoon session—the kids had already been drilling for about seven hours between the morning and afternoon workouts—the kids were dragging their feet. The coaches were running two offenses against the first-string defense, fresh-men included. John was one of the running backs.

"We had some seventy kids out there all hooting and hol-lerin' and running the plays," says Zitoli. "And I noticed John was really dragging it. As he came by me, I said, 'John! Move your ass.' 'F— you,' he fired back. There was dead silence. I mean, you did not do that in that program. I went over to the huddle and grabbed him by the face mask, pulled him in close, and said, 'Don't you ever talk to me that way—I'll knock your effing head off.' And I shoved his head a little."

The head coach got between them, and everyone cooled off. When the session ended fifteen minutes later, Zitoli walked over to John, who was standing next to the head coach.

"Coach. I'm just so tired," John said to Zitoli. "I've got blisters. I'm not in good shape. I'm dying. I'm so sorry I said that to you."

"Okay, John," Zitoli responded. "Please don't ever talk to me that way again. I'll always take care of you."

That was it, Zitoli thought. A heated moment. An apology. Lesson learned. The kids went back to their cabins. Ten minutes later, two captains raced up to the coaches. "John's been hurt. John's hurt," they cried. The coaches rushed to his side. He was in agony. One of the senior boys had decided to take it upon himself to teach John that no one talked to a coach that way. He'd slammed him to the ground and dislocated his elbow.

"It's one of the most painful injuries you could ever have," says Zitoli, who spent some fifteen hours at Hyannis Hospi-tal with John, who was pumped with painkillers while he was waiting for a specialist to arrive. "It was so busy in there I actu-ally had to help set his arm, because there were no nurses avail-able to do it," he recalls. "When I tell you he was in agony, he was in agony." Three surgeries later, it was clear John would never straighten out his arm again.

Zitoli kept tabs on John at school. "I'd see him every once in a while and ask how he was doing." The hair got longer; the pants got baggier. The following year, back at the summer football camp, the head coach called the team together one night. "Fellas," he said, "John took his own life."

Zitoli was grief stricken, but it was not until several years later, when he recounted this wrenching story during an anti-bullying talk he gave at a conference, that he fully realized what he had done. When he finished talking, a woman came up to him and pointed out that by berating John publicly, in front of his teammates—after the boy had cursed at him—Zitoli had inadvertently sanctioned the violent peer bullying that took place later that night. "It started with you," she said. "You bullied the boy first."

How Do I Avoid Inappropriate Adult Talk?

On the ride home from my child's game, I often find myself unable to stop from joining in with my child, putting down other players, parents, or coaches. My dad and I used to do it. It was kind of mean but also fun. Then afterward I'd feel uncomfortable about what I said. What can I do about this?

Discussion: First we need to remember the importance of maintaining a degree of separation between ourselves and our kids. As a society, it's no longer that easy to distinguish between what's appropriate in conversations with children as opposed to with adults. You might feel that sharing these off-color observations brings you and your kid closer together, but, in truth, what we do in such moments is teach our child antisocial behavior. What's really happening—and who among us is not guilty of this from time to time?—is that we are helping our child consolidate biases and teaching him how to label and dehumanize other people. The point you are making may be true—"What's wrong with Jenny? She always needs to be the center of attention"—but by reinforcing this with your child, you are teaching him to focus on the negative. It's only one perspective—a limited way of looking at things—and, as a habit, it's a moderate milestone on the road to the formation of a bullying culture.

Solution: If you know you have this tendency, and this kind of unguarded comment gets away from you, show your child in a very simple doable way that you can "make good" on thoughtless comments by having the courage to reframe them. For example, your unguarded comment might be something like, "Yes, what was Coach Coltrane thinking when she called for man-on-man defense at the end of such a tight game? Our zone was working so well!" Okay, so this is not so bad, really, taken in isolation, but so often it is part of a pattern that opens the door for your child to also become negative and disrespectful. You can reframe it with, "Oops, that was a zinger. What I mean is . . . I must find the right moment to ask Coach Coltrane why she switched to man-on-man defense. I'd like to understand her thinking." It's so important to help our kids understand the difference between thoughtless criticism and critical thinking. We've found this method of reframing to be an effective way to shift away from the put-down habit (for more details see "Put-Down and Trash-Talk Strategies" later in this chapter).

If that's too formal for you, you can pause and self-correct out loud. "This is not right, Jake. Imagine if Tony and his parents were saying this about us. We would not like it at all." Children get this and will readjust their thinking, because now you've personalized it for them.

What Can I Do about Trash Talk?

Put-downs, dissing, and trash talk are a big part of my child's team culture. What can I do?

Discussion: You are not alone. This is a societal problem, one that has reached epidemic levels in all sports. Kids imitate the antisocial behavior they see on television, pick up from adults, or witness from older kids at school. Trash talk is an integral part of the bullying, hazing, and teasing cycle. It involves the subtle exclusion of an individual or small group of individuals. It may be socially tolerated, but it shouldn't be.

You mustn't take these put-downs at face value; they do more than just denigrate someone. There's a much bigger issue here. It's a form of social combat that can quickly lead to more dangerous exclusionary behavior. Regardless of whether it's on the court, on the playground, at home, or in a school corridor, it is a form of stylized dehumanization. And, as we mentioned earlier, dehumanization, when left unchecked, can lead to much worse. When child-athletes and their parents dehumanize opponents in youth sports competitions, this "us vs. them" anticommunal behavior opens the door to bickering, brawling, and worse, as has become alarmingly apparent across America in recent years. We see players and parents fight each other, vicious assaults on referees, and, in one extreme case, one parent who killed another during a dispute at a hockey arena. Trash talk really must be nipped in the bud, because it is the first stage in a spectrum of negative behavior that, in its extreme form, can lead to deeply awful antisocial actions.

Why do kids behave this way? They may be imitating others, but the current runs deeper. For one thing, when a child sees that everyone around him is putting people down, he often figures he's better off going on the offensive, too. It becomes a form of self-protection or defensive communication. Kids also assume that by engaging in put-downs and trash talk, they can improve their own social standing. Fast-talking put-down artists look tough and cool and dominant.

Solution: That, of course, is not true. Show us, anywhere, in any sport, a truly respected athlete who trash talks. The leaders—the team captains—are respectful and care about their fellow players; that's why they are admired. Talk to your kids about this. Tell them that the kids who rise through the ranks to become leaders are the ones who care about their teammates and support them rather than undercut them. The trash talkers, on the other hand, eventually end up as loners. Explain to your kids that the trash talkers on their team may appear to be confident but are often insecure underneath all that bravado, and it shows. The more you trash talk, the more you signal to players on your team and other teams that you lack self-confidence.

Be direct with your ten-year-old. He'll get it. Tell him this is not the way to go. In his book *Best Friends, Worst Enemies: Understanding the Social Lives of Children,* Michael Thompson discusses put-downs, exclusion, and bullying as methods to gain popularity. He exposes the myth that such behavior elevates children's stature in group settings. In fact, they are not impressive to anyone. They may be funny or appear to be cool at a given moment, but that kind of behavior does not win them lasting friends.

Kids play sports mostly to have fun and make friends, and trash talk does not lead to deep friendships. It leads to brief, shallow alliances. On a visceral level, when you behave that way, you reveal to your teammates that you are someone who could turn on them, too, at any moment. If a child is disrespectful to players on other teams, kids on his own team will back off. It might seem at first that he's tough and cool, but what he is really showing is that he is unpredictable and can't be trusted. Obviously he has poor personal boundaries. That negativity, if you are his friend, could be turned on you at a moment's notice. All of this might seem like it would go over the head of a typical ten-year-old, but we have found that when asked about this in an age-appropriate way, kids get this; in fact, they *really* get it.

Teach your kids by your own example. It's a powerful one. Go on a family put-down diet. Become aware of your own inadvertent trash talk; we don't realize how we put each other down all the time, whether we are husband and wife or brother and sister. Unfortunately, this becomes a frame of reference for our kids. When you make a slip—which we do, all the time— that's okay. Just reframe your statement in a positive way. We know how tough it is, but keep trying. You can even make a family exercise of it as you note how many times you put each other down without realizing it. Raising this under-the-radar behavior up into consciousness, even when it only involves noticing and pausing when it is done, is powerful.

Put-Down and Trash-Talk Strategies

It's not funny. Do not allow trash talking and put-downs, or teasing of other kids, no matter how funny it may appear in the moment.

Don't let it slide. Talk to your children. Affirm their great efforts to resist put-downs and trash talk. Timing is crucial; wait until there is a good receptive moment to bring it up.

Family values trump team values—every time. There should be no separation between what a kid does out on a playing field—like trash talking—and what you value as a family. So you can say to your child, "We just don't do that."

No middle ground. We, as the adults in our kids' lives, are either part of the problem or part of the solution. The research of Dan Olweus, one of the most respected sociologists in the field of bullying research, shows that unless we interrupt put-downs right when we hear them, the kids making them presume two things: The adult who overheard is on their side, and the adult is giving *them* permission to escalate the behavior.

Strategy One: Crossing the Line—Accountability without Blame

How many times have we heard a kid say, "But I was only joking around!" Often something may start off kind of funny, but it can easily escalate into something hurtful to another child. Seldom does anyone mean to be mean, but the fact is that it happens.

An effective way of improving your kid's social relationships with others and freeing him up to concentrate on having fun and getting better at his game is to proactively work out the difference between "having fun" and "creating fear."

Here's what the exercise looks like:

1. Sit down with your child and tell him that you want to help him have the most fun possible in the game, and that you understand that "joking around" can often go

too far. Maybe tell him about times in your own life when you crossed the line without meaning it.

2. Ask your child to finish the following sentence in as many ways as possible. (You can then refer back to this when something gets a little edgy and you need to talk.) "Joking around crosses the line and becomes a put-down when . . . " For example, (1) when someone asks you to stop and you don't; (2) when you see that you have offended someone.

Strategy Two: Preview and Review—Sweat the Small Stuff

Seldom does a one-off talk with your child change behavior. Just as a healthy body needs regular moderate exercise, so does healthy social behavior.

Preview. If your child is struggling with put-downs and yet deep down you know that speaking and acting this way is not who she really is, chances are she knows it, too. If you have had a good talk with her and used the "Crossing the Line" strategy, take a brief moment before your daughter goes into the game or the practice and remind her of what she has told you about "the line." Assure her that you believe in her and know she will do her best not to dis and use put-downs.

You might say, "Justine, come over here for a second. Remember that thing about trash talking? Remember what we said? Joking around *crosses the line* and becomes *trash talking* when it deliberately points out another person's weakness. Have a great game, but keep this in mind. I know you can do it." Say it lightly but mean it.

Review. When you are in the car on the way home after practice or a game, take the opportunity to say, "So Justine, how did it go with 'the line' tonight? When did you get close?"

Be as interested in when the line was close or even crossed as you are in successes. No judgment and no cross examination. If we get the response "OK," we usually say, "Great, what was particularly OK? When did you get close to the line?" We like to think of this as being a big heart with ears.

Strategy Three: Disapprove–Affirm–Discover–Do Over (DADD)

An everyday tool for working with children's arguments, put-downs, and trash talk, this strategy can be used to deal with a simple clash between children, or when a put-down has taken place at training or in a game. It can be used over the space of days when the issue is more complex. The aim of learning this strategy is that when the children need help, you will be able to intervene with quiet confidence without seeming to be on anybody's side. That way, you avoid a defensive reaction. Because only one out of every ten put-downs is actually witnessed by adults, it's important to speak up when the opportunity presents itself. When we remain silent, we implicitly condone the behaviors we witness.

Disapprove. First, begin by expressing clear disapproval for the action: "It is hurtful to behave as you did. We don't speak that way in our family/team." Speak with quiet directness. Mean it.

Affirm. We know that we are supposed to separate a child's actions from his/her whole being, but it's not always easy. To achieve this, your disapproval needs to be followed up right away by an affirmation: "You hardly ever speak like that. So often you say helpful things."

Discover. Later, when the time is right, find out what the underlying issue is. "What's up? Something must be bothering you." Or, "Okay, I get it. It's hard not to do it because everybody seems to speak like this." This question must come at the right time to elicit an honest response.

Do over. Finally, when the issue is clarified, you can help the child to do it over. "Let's work out a way you can be a part of the game without speaking that way," or "What are the ways you can be a part of the good stuff but not join in with the put-downs?"

Considering your child's temperament is the last and very important component to this new regime, if it is to work for a particular child. Timing is all important in DADD practice, and there are few better ways to get this right than to know your child's temperament. If you're unsure, try asking yourself, "Which of the following temperaments best describes my child?"

The **strong/choleric** (ambitious, assertive, prone to mood swings) needs to be spoken to away from friends and usually after he has calmed down. Key words: defer, deflect until you can be direct.

The **sensitive/melancholic** (introverted, thoughtful, self-reliant, perfectionist) needs to be spoken to with an understanding of the vulnerability she often experiences. Key words: safety, empathy with quiet accountability.

The **easygoing/phlegmatic** (relaxed, calm, sluggish, passive-aggressive) can become very stubborn if he feels his side has not been heard. Don't take him by surprise. Let him know, for example, that when you are home, you will want to understand why he is speaking in that way. Key words: fairness and timing.

The **flighty/sanguine** (impulsive, pleasure seeking, charismatic, forgetful) needs to be tackled right there and then. If you don't, she will wonder what you are bothering about ten minutes later. Key words: implications of actions.

Why Can't My Child Be Team Captain?

My ten-year-old daughter does not understand why she hasn't been named team captain in the past four seasons. The other day in the car, on our way home from practice, she asked me what exactly was the role of a team captain. She wants to know why she can't be one. "They pick the same three girls as captains every season," she says. "Jody because she's the coach's daughter, Kathy because she scores the most goals, and Samantha because she's Jody's best friend."

Discussion: Teams do not need designated captains before high school age. In youth sports, captain roles are sometimes assigned to stroke the egos of "star players" and sons or daughters of team coaches. By naming captains, coaches set up an unnecessary and divisive hierarchy on teams at a time when children are very sensitive to distinctions. We don't need entitled prima donnas. Coaches should strive to create a strong sense of team equality in younger kids. The role of a captain is to be the liaison between coach and team as well as a leader by example. Younger kids cannot be expected to properly carry out such a function until they have reached the age of fifteen or sixteen.

Coaches may claim they select captains democratically by staging team votes, but the kids who are elected tend to fall into one of three categories: the most popular kid; the best player; a child who is overly dominant or bullies. Few people would agree that popularity, performance, and aggressiveness epitomize the qualities necessary for truly good leadership.

Solution: We have to stop thinking of kids as adults. Although there are kids on youth teams with leadership potential, they may not yet be ready to meet such responsibilities. They are still too young. The coach needs to be the leader on youth teams. If he is not, it can open a leadership void that can make the kids confused as to who is giving them direction. A *Lord of the Flies* scenario can then come about, with the kids prematurely and inappropriately stepping into a role that is beyond their developmental ability. It's important that coaches develop leadership qualities in all players without labeling specific kids. This is a time to sow the seeds of leadership.

If your child's team always appoints captains, approach the coach before he begins the selection process. Ask him or her to reconsider and explain your concerns. If a coach insists that captains are a team or league requirement, suggest that the role be shared by all team members. Rotate the captaincy from game to game and make the designation mean something. It shouldn't simply be a license to show off an armband or a chance to call the coin toss. Ask the coach to give the captain(s) of the week a bona fide leadership task so kids can get a clear picture of what being a leader is really about. For example, the week's designated captains can lead team warm-ups at every practice and prior to the week's game, they can be in charge of equipment, or they can choose a theme that applies to a goal the team sets out to achieve each week (like teamwork, sportsmanship, or commitment). The captains can lead team discussions about the theme at practices and before the week's game. The team can wear the theme as a message on their uniforms or helmets, or post it in the dugout or on the bench as a reminder of their efforts to achieve a collective goal. That way, kids learn that team captaincy is an important, challenging role, not just a glorified label.

Does It Create a Sense of Entitlement When My Kid Wears His Jersey to School?

My son's travel team coach wants the team to wear their jerseys to school. Is this appropriate?

Discussion: Not really, and here's why: A healthy youth sports experience is based on participation and enjoyment, not the need for recognition. Playing on a team should be reward enough. We have to be careful to not promote a look-at-me, I'm-better-than-you attitude. The coach may be trying to foster team allegiance or boost team pride (he also may be using your kids as walking billboards to advertise his elite program to other parents). But the bottom line is that wearing one's uniform at nonteam events can risk promoting a sense of entitlement among team members. It can also alienate kids who did not make the team. Whether it's a club team or an elementary or high school squad, cliques and bullying are a major modern-day concern. It's best to avoid them.

Solution: If a coach feels that wearing uniforms outside of games and practices is important to achieving team unity (and let's face it, kids love receiving and wearing their team duds), you can suggest a more effective team-uniform-wearing bonding strategy. Arrange for the team to don its jerseys while engaging in a community service project: The team can clean up a park, help conduct a practice for younger kids, or volunteer at a charity road race. That way, the team is not setting itself apart from others but blending in and developing a sense of community.

Is It Harmful for My Child to See So Much Sports Violence on Television?

What can I do about the alarming things my kids see while watching sports on television? The brutal one-on-one fights in NHL games. The baseball brawls. All the taunting and bad sportsmanship on display.

Discussion: According to the Kaiser Foundation, children are exposed to an average of seven and a half hours of screen media per day. If they are sports fans, then a good amount of that is likely to be sports programming, which often broadcasts socially combative behavior. Many of the regular television shows they watch also convey the same messages. If you are worried about your kids trash talking or bullying, you can't just look at the symptoms but instead need to examine the root causes. To a large extent, they are imitating what they see. To them this appears to be the social norm.

We lay down the law for our kids. We say, "In our family, we don't tolerate this kind of behavior." But then, right in the center of our homes, we have a device of disrespect set up like an altar, in the center of the living room, with all the chairs in the room facing it like church pews. It can appear to be a holy sanctum of disrespect. Televisions can be communicators of disrespect, exposing our children to all kinds of inappropriate behavior.

It's a serious dilemma. We all want respectful homes, and yet the televisions and computers in our homes purvey mixed content, much of which models put-downs and other types of combative communication. As parents, most of us struggle with this. We want courteous and considerate kids, but television and media are also an integral part of our lives. So what can we do about it?

Solution: The answer is quite simple: Seriously consider limiting the amount of media your child consumes. The less they see, the less likely they are to mimic negative behavior. Two issues often come up when we make this suggestion.

One is from parents who say they bond with their kids when watching sports on television. "Watching the World Series with my kids is an important family ritual." Or: "My son and I bond over Sunday NFL games." We are not suggesting you never sit down with your child and watch a ball game. What we are recommending is that you limit the amount they watch, and sit with them and be prepared to explain issues that arise in today's adult sports culture, like fights and unsportsmanlike conduct. But we will restate the obvious: Your kid will get a ton more enjoyment, benefit, and affirmation if you head over to the park together to play catch for a few hours, rather than remain side by side on the couch, watching adults play sports.

The other issue parents often bring up is the challenges they face when trying to control their kids' media consumption. "I'm all for limiting screen time in our home," one parent told us. "We've already taken steps. The kids are only allowed to watch one game and two movies per week. But when we go on vacation or to friends' or relatives' houses, the tube is always on, and they gravitate toward it. We'd rather they were playing sports outside."

In such situations we parents have to distinguish between our sphere of influence and our sphere of concern. What is under your influence? Where can you directly take action and be effective? Your sphere of influence is your home. It's where you set the rules, so you can limit screen time there effectively. Out in the world it's much harder. Screens are everywhere. They are in gas stations, waiting rooms, airports, and restaurants. You can tell friends and relatives that you don't want your children exposed to too much media, and they may respect that, but often you just can't control what goes on beyond your home. The important thing is that you are limiting the negative sports images and behavior they are exposed to at home and telling them why. The message they receive when they are with you goes a long way.

We seldom think about the fact that almost all the games kids watch on television are played by adults, and these adults, whom the kids idolize and emulate, often exhibit antisocial behavior. They taunt each other, fight, and succumb to explosive temper tantrums. We take steps to keep our children from watching movies about intimate relationships between adults since we wouldn't want them to emulate such scenes in their interactions with family and friends, but they are just as susceptible to modeling the poor behavior manifested in adult sports events. If we want them to play freely and creatively with other kids instead of mimicking grown-up athletes, we have to limit their exposure to such imagery. We have lost track, as a society, of the fact that kids are not adults. Little kids shouldn't play adult-oriented games, and they shouldn't watch hours and hours of adult sports, either.

Among the thousands of parents we've asked, "What is your golden memory from childhood?" one of the most common answers is, "Playing with my dad [or mom] in the park." The answer always centers around connection—connection to family, to friends, to nature, and to self. When playing sports, we create and nurture these bonds. Watching somebody else play is just not the same.

What if My Child Wants to Play the Same Position as the Coach's Child?

My son wants to play quarterback on his town youth football team. The coach's son also covets the position. Some of the dads say my son should forget about playing quarterback if he wants to be on the team. I'm guessing this issue comes up often in youth sports. Is there a way to overcome the monopoly of key positions and playing time by a coach's son or daughter?

Discussion: You are absolutely right. Favoritism is pervasive and affects thousands of young athletes in every sport. Quite a few dads sign up to coach so they can choose what they want for their kids. Is it right? No, but on the other hand, they donate considerable time and energy to coaching the whole team for an entire season. Many such coaches are very good and, in all other respects, fair with other kids on the team, but you are likely correct in assuming that your son is at a distinct disadvantage.

Solution: There are several ways to deal with this situation. One is to approach the coach and ask him if your son and other players could possibly share the position—a quarterback rotation of sorts. What often happens is that the coach will tell you what you want to hear. He'll assure you that he will do everything he can to divide playing time at the quarterback position fairly. It may work out that way, and if so, great—but it doesn't always.

It's best to sit down with your son to discuss the situation. Be candid: On a team in which the coach's son is the first-string quarterback, there is no guarantee that your son will get to play the position on a regular basis. Explain to him that he'll come across favoritism and adversity often on his journey through sports and later on in life as well. Suggest that he always have a backup plan or two in case what he wants most does not work out.

Ask him why he wants to play quarterback and if there are other positions he would like to try. Listen carefully to his answer. If you sense that he wants to be a team leader, explain to him that there are other leadership positions on a football team. He could be a defensive captain, for example. On the other hand, if his response suggests he's fixated on being the star of the team, then it's important to point out that sports are not about stars but team play.

As a capable young athlete, he is probably well equipped to play other pivotal, demanding positions. He can train as a running back, a wide receiver, or a defensive back. Make it clear to him that the road to success as a quarterback (or pitcher or point guard) is paved with a wide range of experiences, playing numerous positions in his sport of choice throughout his developmental years. He can make it his ultimate goal to play quarterback, but he should concentrate on learning to play every position well before he specializes. If his desire to play quarterback persists, have him attend an off-season camp or clinic that provides quarterback training. That way he will have an opportunity to play the position and decide if he wants to pursue it further.

There is an alternative setup that would benefit your son or daughter much more than the current typical approach to coaching sports like football. It's a top-to-bottom solution that eliminates youth sports problems like favoritism and early specialization at designated positions. At Whole Child Sports, we believe that every youth sports program should ensure that kids are taught to play every position in the sport they are learning.

In fact, there is really no intrinsic value to setting positions at a young age. As Scott emphasizes in his book *Fair Play,* we should not "pigeonhole kids into one particular position because of their physical size or ability. In order to provide each participant a full experience and an appreciation for the game that lasts a lifetime, you should teach each player every position. If kids are taught the fundamentals of each position, over time they will find the position where they belong naturally, rather than having an adult dictate where they play."

Practices and games should be restructured to allow every kid to have a go at quarterback, center, and wide receiver. Otherwise we run into the old performance-is-paramount brick wall. The mind-set of a coach in a hypercompetitive league is: "I want to win games. If I want to win games, there is no way I'm going to rotate my best quarterback out of such a key position, just so that his teammates get a chance to experience it." The problem is that he's zeroed in on the wrong goal: winning. The ultimate goal of youth sports is to provide kids with positive educational experiences. The only thing we should be obsessed with is *teaching.*

It's time to stop measuring success in runs, touchdowns, goals, or baskets. Every kid should learn to execute plays at every position. In youth sports you are only truly successful as a coach when everyone on your team, and in your entire league, for that matter, experiences improvement in all aspects of the sport, regardless of their athletic ability.

Kids know when they are being treated fairly, and they really enjoy taking a crack at every position. We are not simply suggesting this as a philosophical ideal; we have to put it into practice. When he launched the National Football League's Junior Player Development Program, Scott tested this principle with thousands of kids, and the response was unanimous: The kids loved trying everything out. They had a fun, well-rounded football experience. If we aren't blinded by performance anxiety, our children won't be as susceptible to it either. As they get older, they will find just the right role to play.

• • •

We can all empower ourselves to stand firm against the bullying, trash talk, and favoritism that can discolor our kid's sports experiences. In earlier chapters we talked about stepping back and giving children the space to play more freely, to work out the rules of their games and solve their own conflicts. It is so important for them to develop these social muscles as they grow up. But as we've explained in this chapter, parents and coaches must—yes, must—intercede resolutely whenever dehumanizing behavior like bullying and trash talk takes hold on our fields or courts or playgrounds. If we don't intercede, we tacitly condone such conduct. There is no place for such corrosive behavior in youth sports. This is, after all, a world into which we release our children but over which we can still exercise some positive influence.

In the next chapter, we explore the role of the parent as a child's first coach. It is so important to begin your child's sports journey by her side, ready to step in whenever she and her friends need you. Your primary role as her first coach is not to "train" or "develop" her athletically, but to connect with her, to share active experiences, and to watch over her as she discovers the wonders of sports. At the onset of this journey, no sports experience is required, just care and attention.

CHAPTER 6

You Are Your Child's First Coach— Freeing Your Child from Oppressive, Hyperorganized Sports

From the moment they are born, we guide our children along life's wondrous, rocky path, shepherding them lovingly through the vulnerable early stages of their development. We help them navigate daily physical and emotional challenges and nurture and harbor them as they gradually gather the strength and skills to function on their own. We try our best to shield our toddlers from negative influences in a tumultuous, ever-changing world and praise them often to buoy their self-esteem. We do this because we want them to venture beyond the loving boundaries of family life with self-confidence and determination. We do this because, as parents, we are our children's first coaches.

As our children grow into physically active, upright beings and we introduce them to sports, we pass the coaching baton to others, hopeful that while playing sports with their peers, our kids will be taught new skills, make friends, and develop a passion for exercise. We want them to embrace the social positives of playing competitively with others because we believe that youth sports will provide an environment where they can have fun and develop in a healthy way. We are seldom prepared for what can happen next.

Many of us are swept up in a seductive swirl of expectations and dreams of success and even stardom. Though we truly mean to shield our kids from physical and emotional stress, we may inadvertently thrust them into a fast-paced, pressure-filled arms race: a toxic youth sports culture that can sometimes catch us all up in a fervor of comparison and competition, a culture that promotes early induction of children into expensive travel teams and encourages sports specialization at too early an age. Carried away by this current, we risk becoming something unrecognizable, even to ourselves—judgmental, stressed-out, win-at-all-costs fanatics. As one parent said, "Jimmy really needs to work on his three-point stance. We've hired a private coach so that he has every chance of making the elite squad when he turns ten."

Is this what we as a society, or individually, really want? To shove our kids down such a narrowly defined pathway to achievement? Haven't we lost sight of our original intention—to expose our kids to fun, educational activities? Why do we become so vested in that gleaming trophy we hope to see them hold at the end of tournament weekend? We know this is not the only thing that truly mattered to us—and them. Wide-eyed and eager to please, our children absorb all the antics and overly zealous behavior of parents, teammates, and coaches caught up in this performance hoopla. The obvious risk is that the wrong message sinks into their impressionable minds: that success is measured in victories and championships, not skill development and teamwork. What we are trying to avoid is the mixed message that Mom and Dad love you no matter what, but they are happier if you win. They are excited and even thrilled if you win. Kids get it.

In this chapter we explore a parent's role in developing and tailoring a child's early sports experiences as his or her first coach. Just as more and more parents today are seeking alternatives for their children in education, from homeschooling and charter and voucher schools to retooling curricula in public schools, we believe parents are ready to explore alternatives in youth sports. In this vein we rethink the rules and structures of adult-oriented organized sports and provide parents with guidance so that they may home-coach their children and also form communities of like-minded parents who want to provide their kids with healthier sports experiences. We offer suggestions for exercises, activities, and programs that are fun and developmentally appropriate for younger kids.

This chapter focuses predominantly on Stage One (five- to eight-year-olds) and Stage Two (nine- to eleven-year-olds) of the Whole Child Sports developmental continuum (see "Finding a Road Map to Change with a Focus on Developmental Stages" in chapter 1). Whole Child Sports encourages parents to introduce children ages five to eleven to fun games that develop their movement skills, balance, and coordination (the skills outlined in Stages One and Two). These are not outcome-oriented competitive games; the emphasis is on fun and skill development. We strongly recommend "home sports schooling" for this age group and offer specific examples of backyard games and park activities that can help develop balance and movement skills, as well as creative thinking, but are fun focused and don't require too much adult involvement and direction.

When kids reach the threshold age of eleven or twelve, the time comes for parents to let go a little bit and entrust their children's athletic development to more experienced guides (Stage Three: twelve- to fifteen-year-olds). We do not advocate handing your child over to just anyone, however; choosing the right coach and sport or sports for your child is truly important. Helping children develop speed, balance, and agility can set them on course to enjoy years of wholesome activities as they grow into healthy, happy, accomplished athletic young men and women.

What if I Have No Prior Coaching Experience?

I like the idea of being my child's first coach, but I have no experience whatsoever. How do I do it?

Discussion: Your child is embarking on a movement experience. It's experimental, and you can discover the wonders of sports alongside your child. You don't have to be an expert or pretend to be one. Kids under the age of twelve, and particularly nine or younger, want, more than anything else, to share experiences with their parents. If you express interest in engaging in an activity with them and spend time learning and playing with them, that's all that matters. After the age of twelve or thirteen, kids do seek a balance between interest and expertise. That's okay. You can call in an expert then.

Kim recalls a father he observed in his hometown of Northampton, Massachusetts. "The dad could hardly throw a ball. But he could put a mitt on, and his son loves pitching. So they're out there for an hour every evening playing catch. The son's this big kid who pitches really well. The dad's a little on the 'nonathlete' side of the spectrum. But there they are every day—a dad and his ten-year-old kid. Having fun."

Play, games, and sports are all about developing connections. If you are willing to get out there, put on a mitt, and catch your son's fastball, that's all that counts. The connection is what matters at this stage, not skills. As your child's first coach, you play a central role in his future athletic development. One key ingredient in any child's sports biography is the "passion to play." Fun is the foundation on which long-term participation and success in sports are built. You can foster this in your child no matter how little experience you have as a coach or player.

If you introduce your child to the joy of sports, it makes a lasting impression on him. As his appreciation grows, he will be much less likely to drop out down the line. Learning a sport requires discipline: Plenty of practice and repetition are needed to develop skills and hone techniques. If you have cultivated a passion for play in your young play-oriented athlete, however, he or she will want to work through the more difficult stages of skill development.

Solution: Whether it's something as simple as soccer basics or as complex as a golf swing, there are dynamic ways to introduce every sport to any child. Take golf, for example: If your kid expresses an interest in the game and you've never played it before, don't rush to sign him up for lessons. His smaller hands, fragile ego, and developing neural circuitry are not appropriate for the adult version of this challenging game. Play fun golf-like games with him at home or in the park instead.

Golf is a sport that requires a great deal of technique. Most parents don't have the knowledge or skills to teach it to their children, but they can certainly find dynamic ways to introduce the basics. Here are a number of ways you can provide an enjoyable golfing experience without overburdening a child with instruction:

Frisbee golf (ideal for Stages One to Four). It's not the traditional game using clubs, but it does replicate the scoring methods, the challenges of shot making, and strategy. The toss of a Frisbee actually replicates several of a golf swing's key components: shifting weight from the back to the front foot, upper body rotation, and follow-through. Frisbee golf can be set up in your backyard, at a local park, or, for the more advanced, in park trails. Precision and shot making are keys to this game. If you have plenty of room, set up eighteen different holes, using trees or poles as holes or targets. Or you can purchase metal baskets that sit off the ground on their own poles. If you have limited space, set up as few as three holes of three different lengths and degrees of difficulty (around corners or over shrubs) and play each set of three holes six times. As par for each hole, assign a designated number of shots the average player should take to hit the hole or target. To score your round, add up the number of shots it takes to complete each hole.

Backyard golf (Stages Two to Four). This is a game Scott played in his backyard throughout his childhood, while imagining himself to be Jack Nicklaus, Gary Player, or Ben Crenshaw.

(Okay, so now Scott has revealed his vintage.) Players use real clubs (a seven iron and/or pitching wedge will do), often cut down to a more appropriate length, with either plastic golf balls (small wiffle balls) or short-flight foam balls. Targets can be tree trunks, pails, and even Hula-Hoops. Or you can splurge and purchase portable golf targets (such as those made by BirdieBall).

Snag golf (Stages One and Two). With this more expensive option, you can replicate different types of shots while limiting the frustration that comes with missing them too often. It helps make playing fun and is easy to use. The larger plastic club heads and tennis-like Velcro balls help you create an experience that is less challenging for young acolytes. The targets are different forms of colorful bull's-eyes positioned horizontally or at ground level. When the balls make contact, they stick to the Velcro surfaces.

Is It Better for My Child to Play a Team Sport or an Individual Sport?

I love seeing my child involved in individual activities, but I don't want to raise an antisocial child. I want my kid to learn to be a good team player. Should I be concerned that he seems more oriented toward individual sports?

Discussion: This may sound obvious, but, for starters, it's important to note that kids have different temperaments. Outgoing kids are drawn to team sports, like football or basketball, while more introverted children tend to want to participate in individual sports, such as tennis or golf, if they want to play competitive sports at all. This is not a hard and fast rule, but it is surprising how often it is the case.

Solution: You can interest introverted kids in an array of sports, but it's best—at least at the start—for the sport to be a little quieter and less hectic than, say, baseball or football, which involve large, boisterous groups of kids. A sport like tennis can serve as a social bridge for a typically quieter and somewhat introverted child. It's individually oriented, but when he plays, he interacts with an opponent and is part of a squad with a few teammates.

One thing's for certain: There is absolutely nothing wrong with sticking with individual sports if your child feels more comfortable with them. If sports like golf or tennis don't fit the bill, dial it a back a bit further and start with more solitary activities like climbing, running, canoeing, or hiking.

Be sure to join in if you can. Use the activity as a pathway to develop and strengthen your connection with your child. Peruse hiking magazines and trail books with him. Help him pack his backpack. Introverted kids usually want, and probably can only handle, a few more-intimate connections and friendships. You can help expand your child's social world a bit by doing activities with him, and then inviting one or two kids who also like the activity to join him. Keep it small and intimate but not isolated.

Another thing to consider: Your child may be seeking life balance. If his life is pressured and hectic, he could be gravitating toward solitary activities as a self-protective, life balancing measure in order to find an oasis of calm. If that's the case, go with it. Help facilitate such activities, and also look for ways you can help simplify his outer life so that he feels less pressured. That may lead him to seek more engagement with others.

How Can I Foster My Child's Athletic Potential?

Every kid has athletic potential. How do I nurture and develop the athlete in my child?

Discussion: Most children have been served up an unhealthy diet of too much screen time (television, computers, smartphones, video games) and too little "free play." One result: potentially delayed development of motor skills. That's why it's so important to get your child moving. Whether it's in the basement, the backyard, or the park, your child needs to be running, jumping, bumping, throwing, and catching as much as possible.

Solution: Awakening your child's inner athlete is actually easy to do and can be really fun for both of you. But before you begin, there is one ironclad rule you must keep in mind: Do not overburden your child with instruction. Kids tune out their parents (and coaches) if they are bombarded with ideas, suggestions, and corrections. If you are teaching your child a game or technique, correct her only once or twice each outing. There's plenty of time for adjustments. If you overcorrect, you become a killjoy. To be honest, we all get excited and can be overbearing at times.

Create an area of your home (inside or out) that encourages experiential play and self-discovery. Set up fun zones that encourage jumping, running, throwing, and catching. Sometimes leaving a ball out near a colorful target is all it takes for a child to begin experimenting on his own.

Set up an obstacle course that requires different movement skills: crawling under; jumping over; kicking; running through and around obstacles. Once your child has mastered the course, you can add a self-measuring element, such as timing how fast she gets through the course.

Be sure to include balance as a play option. It's one of the most important, often forgotten, elements of athletic development today. (Balance games and equipment are outlined later in the chapter.)

Sports Equipment for Your Home Coaching

With these six basic pieces of equipment, you can engage your kids in fun, challenging athletic training at home.

Vew-Do NUB Boards. This safe and fun balance-training device helps a child develop body awareness, core strength, and rotational movement. In addition, the boards replicate board-sports (skateboarding, snowboarding, surfing) movements. These boards are fractions of an inch off the ground, so they do not easily slip out from under the child (appropriate for Stages Two to Four).

Pitchback. No backyard should be without a pitchback. They can be used for solo games of catch (baseball and lacrosse) and as throwing and kicking targets. Create dozens of fun games and skill competitions with a pitchback to develop hand and foot/eye coordination in conjunction with agility training (Stages One to Three).

Agility ladder. Use the ladder to develop agility, balance, and coordination in hundreds of movement drills and obstacle course configurations. The ladder is laid flat on any solid surface and can be replicated on a driveway area with chalk (Stages Two to Four).

Step2 balance ball. As your child plays with this ball, he develops his balance skills, which leads to improved agility (change of direction, footwork) and better coordination and efficiency of movement. It also strengthens the supporting ligaments and muscles around his ankles, knees, and hips, which can help keep your child playing sports injury free (Stages One and Two).

Frisbees, tennis balls, and NERF balls. There are dozens of ways to incorporate these simple items in engaging drills that develop agility, balance, coordination, and speed. Tennis balls can be used in extensive hand/eye coordination drills for various sports. In fact, they are now used by many top athletic development trainers worldwide. NERF balls (footballs, baseballs, soccer balls, and indoor basketballs) are some of the safest and easiest types of balls to use when teaching throwing, catching, and kicking (Stages One to Four).

Gymnastic mats. A simple gymnastic mat allows your kids to experiment with tumbling, rolling, and falling without fear of seriously injuring themselves. Mats are also great additions to any obstacle course you build in your backyard or home, and they can be used as a safe landing area under any type of balance equipment (Stages One to Four).

Backyard / Local Park Obstacle Course: Fun and Fitness Home Coaching Program (Stages One to Three)

The objective of this course is to provide a dynamic fitness workout that promotes playful experimentation. This obstacle-course activity helps children develop agility, balance, coordination, and body strength. How each child attempts to move through the course can add variety to the training experience. Kids may elect to move laterally, backward, or forward. They may jump, jog, or walk. The basic setup consists of five stations. Each station can be adjusted to increase or decrease the level of difficulty by adding elements or taking props away.

Equipment

The equipment required for this obstacle course:

- 16 banana hurdles (low hurdles) of two or three different heights (six, twelve, and eighteen inches)
- 2 agility ladders
- 10 disc cones
- 6 half-foam rolls (an additional 6 half-foam rolls are added for harder courses)
- 4 pairs of poles, cones, and clips (set up above the half-foam rolls)

Space Requirements

The course takes up approximately 900 square feet. It can be set up in a space as small as 250 square feet, however, by reducing the number of banana hurdles in each row. Each station can be set up and adjusted to suit the training purpose, usage, and age and skill level of the kids.

Dynamic Balance and Multiterrain Station

This particular station, which helps build balance, agility, coordination, and lower body strength, requires more set-up time and attention. The simplest setup includes four sets of poles, clips, and cones arranged at different heights approximately six feet apart. Each participant passes through this station by moving in a squat position under each pole set, maintaining balance without touching the ground with his hands. You'll find photos and video of the setup and execution of this drill at www.wholechildsports.com.

After passing under each set of poles, the participant stands up, continues to move forward without stopping, then immediately lowers himself into another squat position to go under the next pole set. This continues until he has completed the course. All participants should keep their backs straight and torsos upright, taking care not to bend at the waist as they pass under each obstacle in the squatting position. The level of difficulty can be increased by lowering the height of the different pole sets.

In the most advanced version of the station, five banana hurdles are set up between the pole sets, along with four sets of two half-foam roll pairs, which are placed underneath the pole sets and hurdles. The children must move under each obstacle, keeping their balance while stepping over the banana hurdles. Again, the exercise can be made more difficult by lowering the height of the different pole sets.

A third version of this obstacle station can be set up by replacing the pairs of half-foam rolls with a single row. The athlete now has to maintain his balance on the single roll, which is much harder.

In a fourth version of the station, the terrain is altered. The banana hurdles are eliminated and the half-foam rolls are arranged in different directions, requiring participants to readjust their footing while trying to stay balanced.

Can Moms Coach, Too?

I'm a mom, and I don't know much about sports. Everywhere I go, I see mostly men in charge. I'd like to try to coach, but I'm not all that confident. I don't know if I'd be good at it.

Discussion: Becoming a youth coach is not as complicated as it would seem. Yes, it's still primarily a male dominated world, and that may give you pause, but the men you see patrolling the sidelines—clipboards in hand—come from a very mixed bag of sporting backgrounds and successes. What we are politely saying here is that we men can sometimes seem just a little bit more confident than we are competent—not big news to our female readers. You have as much of a right to be coaching kids as any man does. If you enjoy teaching, are semiorganized, and have passion, dedication, and a willingness to learn new things, you are an ideal candidate.

Solution: At Whole Child Sports we believe women are the single greatest underutilized resource in youth sports today. At a time when we clearly need to break the traditional mold of ego-dominated, command-oriented youth sports, a massive influx of eager, dynamic, dedicated female coaches could really help change the way millions of kids experience sports.

In her comprehensive book, *Home Team Advantage: The Critical Role of Mothers in Youth Sports,* Brooke de Lench lists nine reasons why women have the right values for youth sports:

1. Women are natural teachers.

2. Women tend to be less authoritarian leaders.

3. Women are natural nurturers.

4. Women tend to want to find balance between competition and cooperation.

5. Women care about all children, not just their own.

6. Mothers want to protect children from the pressures of the adult world.

7. Women are safety conscious and risk averse.

8. Women are good at teaching boys healthy masculinity.

9. Women coaches are role models for girls and can teach them to celebrate being female athletes.

As a woman and a mother, you have a great deal more to contribute to your children's sports experience than scheduling, carpooling, preparing snacks, and cheering from the sidelines. We know this is obvious, but it still bears mentioning. You can imbue your coaching style with sensitivity to your players' physical and emotional needs, teach them with age-appropriate rather than command-driven attitudes, and nudge them along while shielding them from the soul-damaging focus on winning at all costs that permeates the youth sports system today.

A Mom: A First-Time Coach

Even in the virtually all-male bastion of youth football, women can have a resounding impact at the helm. Consider Xiomara. A thirty-five-year-old divorced mother of two boys, ages six and eight, Xiomara was rooting for Jordan, her eldest, from the sidelines at the start of one football season. Then the team coach dropped out unexpectedly, and she was asked to step in and co-coach with one of the fathers. As the only female coach in her league, Xiomara turned heads. "The opposing coaches thought I was a mommy helper. When they saw me on the field in the huddle with the kids, they did a double take." But that didn't faze her.

"I jumped right in and took the coaching course," she says. "I read everything I could get my hands on." The hardest part for Xiomara, a Yonkers, New York, police officer, was learning to read plays and figure out how her offense and defense should execute them. "That was frustrating," she admits, "but I picked it up as the weeks went by." Whenever she didn't understand something, she asked someone. "The other coaches were really helpful," she says, "though I did get teased a little bit when they saw me carrying my copy of *Coaching for Dummies* everywhere I went."

Xiomara learned everything from the ground up: getting into a stance, positioning in form tackling, and blocking. Once she understood it well enough, she taught her charges. As one parent pointed out, "Other volunteer coaches might think they know the fundamentals, but they don't necessarily. Because Xiomara was starting from zero and didn't have an inflated ego, she learned how to do it right and taught her players well."

Another positive: She communicated well with her boys. "I made sure to repeat myself often when I was going over the fundamentals," she says. "I had to remind the other coaches, 'These are eight-year-olds. They forget.' With their nerves, energy, and excitement, you have to tell them over and over." In the huddle and on the sidelines during games, she'd review the basics again and again. "That was important to me," she says. "Keeping the kids safe. We had no major injuries." The other coaches followed her example.

She nurtured her players and was careful to consider them as individuals. "There were a few boys I figured wouldn't last a week," she says. "I knew they couldn't handle being corrected in public. So I'd whisper in their ears, 'You're doing great. Just keep in mind you have to keep your head up. Keep your eyes up. I don't want you to get hurt.' At the end I fell in love with each and every one of them and was so happy they'd stuck with it."

As the days grew shorter and colder, Xiomara noticed that some kids didn't show up at practice and games with warm enough clothing, so she'd bring extra sweatshirts and put them on her players. "The other coaches would look at me like, 'Really?' And I'd say, 'Keep your mouth shut!'" Hard-nosed old-schoolers might shake their heads, but mommy coach was a big hit. "They came up to me at the awards assembly and said, 'Thank you, Coach, for all the little things you did for us.' It just warmed my heart." But perhaps Xiomara's finest endorsement came from her own son. "I asked, 'Do you want Mommy to coach you next year?' And Jordan replied, 'Yes.'"

Inspired by her experience on the gridiron, Xiomara has now signed up to coach another sport she's never played: basketball. We hope more mommies will follow.

What if My Child Doesn't Want Me to Coach?

My son and daughter don't want me to coach them. How can I be their first coach?

Discussion: First off, you are not alone. Many kids don't want to be coached by their parents, especially as they get older and become more socially integrated with their peers. Don't take it personally. They just want to explore and experience things as individuals.

There are, however, ways to participate in your child's athletic journey—just not in the traditional command-based coaching sense. In fact, more and more, coaches are realizing that command-based coaching is not a very effective way to engage kids. It's best to set up games and activities that develop skill, challenge your child, and involve you as well. Benjamin Franklin's words speak volumes: "Tell me and I forget. Teach me and I remember. Involve me and I learn." So take a cue from some of today's most dynamic youth coaches, who emphasize experiential learning.

Solution: You can guide your child by providing him with opportunities to learn and develop skills without assuming the role of instructor. The trick is to come up with unique, entertaining games that engage him. Skill development should be fun. If your son is having fun, being challenged, and experiencing incremental successes, he will want to play actively more often.

Set up an activity in your yard or at the park. Your children will be drawn to it out of curiosity. It should involve plenty of movement (kids love to run, jump, throw, catch, and crawl) and can be geared toward a sport or activity they've already expressed interest in.

The following are two games Scott set up and played with his son in his backyard.

Receiving/Defending Game

This game requires a pitchback screen or rebounder. You can find one online or at any sporting goods store. They're used primarily with tennis, lacrosse, and baseballs, but the game Scott played with his son involved a NERF football. If you toss a NERF ball against a rebounder, it can send the ball back a good distance in unpredictable directions, making for a dynamic one-on-one receiving/defending game that develops athletic agility (change of direction), hand/eye coordination, and speed. This game is ideal for Stages Two and Three (nine-to fifteen-year-olds).

How to play: Mark off a space of about fifteen yards by ten yards with cones. Place the rebounder in the center of the court. Designate a goal line on each side of the rebounder. Each play begins with one participant throwing the ball into the rebounder and a second player (his opponent) standing next to or behind him. The player throwing the ball must be no more than two yards back from the rebounder. Play begins when the ball is thrown into the rebounder and bounces at least five yards back, where it becomes a free ball. The first player who catches the ball attempts to score past the goal line adjacent to each side of the rebounder. If the player is touched prior to crossing the goal line or the ball drops to the ground, the play is dead. The players switch roles, and the next person throws the ball into the rebounder on the next play.

Scott and his son, eight at the time, played this game together throughout the fall. It was a fun alternative to playing catch, and it captured Scott's son's imagination and challenged him physically.

Balance in Motion Game

All you need for this game is a wooden two-by-four (or two-by-six) about eight to ten feet long, two tennis balls, and one six- and one twelve-inch-high hurdle. It's great for kids in Stages One and Two (ages five to eleven).

How to play: The child walks forward and backward along the beam four times. Then she does so again, but this time she must maintain her balance as she tries to catch tennis balls thrown at her from ten feet away. To complicate things, balls can be tossed from a variety of directions, both in front and behind her and both high and low.

Once she's mastered this, you can have her walk laterally (sideways) by crossing one foot over the other, then stepping to the side, and then crossing the first foot behind the other foot. She should cross the beam and return to the other side, facing the same direction. When this is perfected, she should increase her speed.

To dial up the difficulty, add a six-inch and a twelve-inch hurdle, placed on the ground over the beam, that the child must step over while making her way across. In the final stage, add a partner to the activity. Place two eight- to ten-foot two-by-fours flat on the ground next to each other widthwise. Two kids walk toward each other, starting from opposite ends, and pass without touching or stopping. Once they have done this successfully repeatedly, add tennis ball catching and then hurdle stepping. Finally, when they are proficient, remove one of the two-by-fours and have them try again on a single beam.

Another fun option that Scott's son discovered and developed with his friends consisted of adding more two-by-fours of differing lengths to create longer balance courses. Under Scott's supervision, they designed numerous challenging courses that went under obstacles, such as picnic tables, and over others, like backyard benches and stone walls.

Signs That Your Kid's Coach Is Ego Driven

After judiciously guiding your child through the early stages of her athletic development as her first coach, don't let your guard down. If you encounter a toxic coach, find another coach, team, or sport your child can play that season. You will know this coach is likely ego driven if:

- He overplays certain kids in order to win, seeking a fast-track road to success and showing disregard for safety ("Shake it off; we need you to play"), which misses the point of youth sports, to develop and challenge every child.
- She is loud and draws attention to herself on the sidelines, arguing frequently with and disrespecting officials, forgetting the fact that she is a powerful role model for the kids on her team.
- He speaks more than listens, behaving like a dictator, creating a culture in which parents have to shout to be heard, refusing to discuss schedules with parents, and disregarding family-time concerns.
- She is defensive and confrontational, refusing to acknowledge that others can provide interesting insights and instead seeing them only as opposing opinions.
- He fosters a fear of failure by reacting negatively to mistakes instead of using them as teaching moments.
- She calls kids out inappropriately and repeatedly in front of their peers.
- He demonstrates lack of awareness of his players' individual character traits and temperaments, thereby exposing his own inflexibility.
- She shows that she's never come to terms with her own sports biography, living vicariously through the team's accomplishments, coping poorly with their failures, and

making repeated, unprompted references to her athletic resume and coaching accomplishments.

- He fails to recognize that a lot can be learned by listening to parents, since they know their own child best.

- She can't differentiate the team dynamic from individual personalities and fails to see the importance of the social dynamic of the team.

- He overpraises the kids, which undermines their true accomplishments, and confuses praise with affirmation, creating praise junkies and a watch-me dependence that leads to cynicism or a prima donna syndrome.

- She exhibits rigidity and an unwillingness to move beyond her own comfort zone, failing to realize a coach should be constantly learning about the sport she coaches and the kids she teaches.

Choosing a Coach:
A Parent's Checklist

While you will always need to remain active in guiding your child's sports life, at some point you will pass on the coaching baton to more experienced individuals. Finding a good coach for your kid is important—and not always easy. As you search, keep these questions in mind:

❏ Does the coach encourage fair play and emphasize honor and self-control?

❏ Does she place more emphasis on winning or participation? Is she willing to select the players who give their best for the team as opposed to those who are gifted but may be selfish and unreliable?

❏ Is he aware of the social dynamic in the group and can he relate on a deeper level to some of the issues he may be confronted with? Is he active in organizing social as well as sporting events for the team and their friends and families?

❏ Is she a good role model? Your son or daughter may identify strongly with the way the coach lives. Are you comfortable with this?

❏ Does he overtrain or overexert the players?

❏ Does she take winning and losing personally and transfer her frustrations onto the players?

❏ Does he encourage positive self-image of all players and affirm their strengths as well as attempt to improve their weaknesses?

❏ Does she give too much attention to the "star" of the team, neglecting the others?

❏ Is he willing to relate to, and not exclude, the parents of the players?

CHAPTER 7

And in All Things . . . Balance and Flow

For two months each summer, Cooperstown, New York, hosts one of the largest national youth baseball tournaments in the United States. More than one hundred teams descend on this sleepy town each week to test their mettle at the Cooperstown Dreams Park facility.

Sounds like a great event for kids! Thousands of boys age twelve and under face off on pristine fields and board in cozy barracks; their families occupy the local hotels and team up to share rented homes, and their siblings horse around with other kids who aren't playing. To add to the hoopla, there's a team visit to the Baseball Hall of Fame and state pins that players and siblings collect and trade. Could there be a more idyllic setting for a youth sports tournament?

John Harding, father to three boys, figured it would be the quintessential American family vacation. His eldest, Tommy, was twelve and played on an elite New England–based travel team the summer of the Harding family trip to Cooperstown. "The facility was like Disney, beautifully clean and manicured," John says. They had webcams positioned around the baseball diamonds and broadcast some of the games on the Internet, so

149

grandparents and other family members could log on and watch. We had some really emotional moments, like come-from-behind victories and the two double plays my son helped execute."

You don't have to dig too deep to discover that big business is also at play here. Hundreds of thousands of parents each spend thousands of dollars at similar tournaments across the country. Youth sports tourism is a full-blown industry. Complexes like the one in Cooperstown have popped up in dozens of small towns across America, and more are in the works. "The amount of money everyone spends is incredible," says John. "Some teams flew in from Hawaii and North Dakota." This one event, which lasts only eight weeks, costs approximately ten thousand families over $30 million, though it accounts for less than 1 percent of the total baseball-playing youth population. Youth sports, in general, cost families well over $5 billion each year.

When you factor in the time spent traveling to and participating in these tournaments; the emotional cost to kids who arrive with outsized expectations and win-at-all-cost mindsets; and the time spent in controlled environments where untrained volunteers make decisions that directly affect your child's self-esteem, friendships, and athletic development, you begin to wonder whether this is the best setup for your child. Youth sports is big business, and businesspeople capitalize on the misguided expectations of parents and kids who pin all their hopes on advancing to the next level. Just think of what could be done if those same team parents pooled even a fraction of this money and invested it in improving youth sports activities within their own communities. (See "Five Better Ways to Invest in Your Kid's Athletic Future—Locally" on page 161.)

Children do make some good memories at these tournaments, but, for the most part, their time is not spent with you. They're in barracks every night with their teammates and coaches, and when you realize how tightly focused many coaches are on winning, you have to wonder what exactly is being discussed with your kids—especially since you are not present to provide some perspective. These coaches may be well-meaning volunteers, but, for the most part, they have limited coaching training and little understanding of child development.

Such tournaments also consume many designated family vacation days, and recreational time is tightly structured around the competition. Most of us have a limited amount of time and money we can allocate to vacations, yet, at Cooperstown, families spend thousands of dollars and dedicate an entire week—for the most part, to one particular child—while the rest of the family sacrifices valuable family time and money. "Cooperstown was an expensive trip," says John. "About $3,000, in all. Times are still tight, so that was our one big vacation for the summer." The players' siblings—some of whom have no affinity for baseball—are dragged from game to game from morning until night to watch their brothers play. "It wasn't all bad for Tommy's brothers," John says. "We rented a house with two other families, and they got to swim in the pool and play with other young kids we invited over." But it wasn't all roses, either. "By midweek the little guys were whining, 'Can we go home now?'"

Such youth sporting extravaganzas underscore how far we've wandered off the path to developing a Whole Child. As if winning a so-called national championship at age eleven is central to a kid's athletic or personal development. Surely the young athlete and the entire family would benefit much more if their limited time and resources were spent relaxing, playing freely, and exploring places they've never been before together.

Each year more than forty million American children participate in organized sports leagues, according to the National Council of Youth Sports. That number has climbed significantly over the past decade. What's troubling is that children are joining these programs earlier than ever, with some organizations assembling teams for children as young as eighteen months old. Says Tom Farrey in *Game On,* "The race to the bottom in youth sports, where there's no such thing as too young, represents one of the most profound—and unexamined—trends of recent decades." Another disturbing fact: Participation peaks at age eleven, just when children are reaching an age when involvement in team sports is developmentally ideal.

Parents should pause and ponder: How does playing in as many organized games as possible each season, and traveling around the country to so-called national championships, benefit our children? Think back to simpler times—your own childhood, perhaps—when games and competitions materialized on street corners and in sandlots in your neighborhood, when you and your friends were in charge of making up the rules, and adult supervision was limited. As we've discussed in previous chapters, we need to strike a balance between organized sports and other all-important play stages in a child's life. Youth sports organizations and parents who have bought into this system have unwittingly displaced important stages of childhood development—the imaginative play stage, unstructured free play, and the semistructured game play period—which means the quality of a child's cognitive, emotional, and physical development is compromised.

It would seem that America has been gripped by a malformed ethos built, as Farrey points out, "around the principle of identifying and promoting . . . the next generation of athlete-entertainers . . . [which] can be found in some form, in virtually every community in which child's play is organized." This mind-set, Farrey adds, "holds that it's never too early to train children as competitors." As a result, some parents, hopeful that their child-athlete might become America's next Olympic phenom, busy themselves building a launching pad that will catapult Team Toddler into the promised land. Big business feeds on such hopes, pumping billions of dollars into advertising and television deals in an effort to glamorize adult or pro sports, which in turn fuels further "professionalization" and "adultification" of child and youth sport activities.

How can we find a better balance for our children in today's society? Where has the balance gone in our own lives when the emphasis in sports has drifted away from simple enjoyment, learning, and improving? Instead, it all seems to be about seeking out the best competitions, and playing the most games year-round, in order to achieve the virtually unattainable goal of superstardom. Statistically speaking, that's a realm reached by a tiny fraction of the sporting population.

Within the Whole Childs Sports organization, our differing viewpoints, backgrounds, and experiences spur us to healthy debate. Should we swing the pendulum all the way back to simpler times, with semiorganized play limited to the confines of our neighborhoods? Should sports stay that way throughout childhood?

Kim's thoughts swing more toward dialing things down, particularly in a child's early years, and even as he and his wife gradually introduce team sports to his daughters, they go the extra mile to find coaches who encourage fun and self-discovery, and they pay close attention to the social climate of the team. Scott grew up with neighborhood play but has participated with his son, and professionally, on the other side of the pendulum, where most Americans choose or are forced to reside. Luis has dabbled in both worlds. He vacations with his family in a secluded, natural setting in Maine, where his kids play naturally and wholesomely, but back in New York they participate in organized sports once or twice a week. As they get older, they will become more involved in such activities. Despite these different backgrounds, all three of us believe that the Whole Child Sports experience should swing as if along the arc of a pendulum at various ages, with a balanced center as our ultimate goal.

At Whole Child Sports, we are dedicated to forging a new path. During the earliest ages of childhood, we recommend simplicity and free play. The pendulum swings toward a balanced center, which is reached when a child is twelve. That balanced center can be maintained for a lifetime, through recreational games and different types of competitive (self-measuring) athletic and fitness-focused pursuits. The center needs to consist of an equal amount of learning and training to improve skills, participation in free and organized play, and involvement in multiple sports. It should represent a wholesome life rhythm in which involvement in sports balances well with a young athlete's other activities and pursuits.

Many kids should and do stay at this recommended center point throughout their teenage years. Others, as they get older, gravitate toward more focused competitive experiences (best at the age of fifteen or older). Kids can always swing back to the

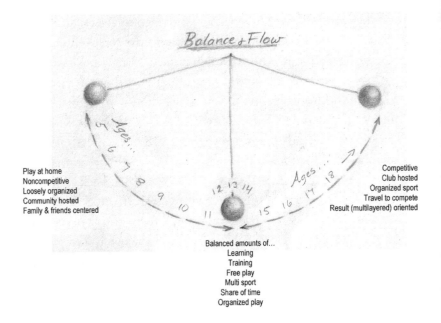

Balance & Flow

Play at home
Noncompetitive
Loosely organized
Community hosted
Family & friends centered

Ages...
5 6 7 8 9 10 11 12 13 14 15 16 17 18

Ages...

Competitive
Club hosted
Organized sport
Travel to compete
Result (multilayered) oriented

Balanced amounts of...
Learning
Training
Free play
Multi sport
Share of time
Organized play

center when they need to rest and recharge, before returning to more demanding competition in high school and beyond, if they so choose.

This chapter covers various aspects of finding and maintaining balance in youth sports: balancing family time and resources with youth sports activities; understanding social and emotional balance in relation to sports; and learning and developing physical balance skills as a key part of laying down a strong, healthy foundation for the young athlete. The chapter concludes with our ten tenets of a balanced Whole Youth Sports experience.

How Can I Manage the Financial Cost of Youth Sports?

I've just added up the amount of money I've spent this year on my kids' sports activities. I'm stunned! And I haven't even factored in the time spent on this. What should I do?

Discussion: We wish we had a silver bullet response to this question, but we don't. Depending on your income bracket, you can easily spend anywhere between $1,000 and $20,000 on your kids' sporting efforts . . . *per year!* Things have certainly gotten out of hand. Luis has four sons. When three of them were just getting into their prime soccer-playing years, Luis reviewed his credit card bill after four trips to the sporting goods store and almost passed out. Each kid had been outfitted in turf shoes and shin guards, got goalie gloves and track suits, as well as sports bags to carry all the stuff they'd just loaded up on. Then he found out that he'd have to double the amount spent on footwear to outfit his sons with the proper shoes to play indoor soccer as well. Keep in mind that this is small potatoes compared with what some parents dole out for their kids to play on "select" or "elite" travel teams.

In checking around, we found blogger Fran Dicari, who runs StatsDad.com. Here's what he spent on his kids in 2011:

Admission fees (running total):	$265
Physical therapy copay (running total):	$75
Golf putter (Rossa White Ghost):	$159
Five sessions with personal coach (baseball):	$250
Baseball metal cleats (Nike Swingman):	$90
Baseball turf shoes (Ignite II Under Amour):	$60
Baseball glove (Wilson A2000 Limited Edition):	$250
Spring/summer AAU basketball fees:	$495

Spring soccer fees:	$100
Soccer trip (Columbus):	$215
Baseball glove restringing:	$28
Mouth guard(s) (Shock Doctor):	$30
Condo baseball tournament:	$1,600
Condo basketball tournament:	$720
Baseball fees (second round):	$500
Tennessee baseball trip:	$460
Girls CYO basketball fees:	$150
Boys CYO golf fees:	$150
Preowned golf clubs (Ping Eye2 irons):	$120
Preowned golf club (Ping R15 driver):	$175
Callaway golf bag:	$100
Airline tickets (travel tournament):	$1,250
Gas to date:	$912
College Conference Challenge trip:	$385
Puma goalie gloves:	$55
Nike Lebron basketball shoes:	$119
Nations Baseball Premier Nat'l Championship trip (excluding condo, paid previously):	$850
Soccer fees:	$550
Golf glove and balls:	$40
Boys fall basketball fees:	$150
Goalie shorts and shirts:	$84
Nike Jordan Independence Day shoes: (my son paid the difference)	$80
Doctor/MRI for elbow:	$150
Personal trainer:	$500
Personal trainer (batting):	$350
Personal trainer (throwing):	$350
Total:	$11,817

Why is Fran Dicari—a Cincinnatti-based advertising executive—plunking down so much cash on youth sports? As he explained to Mark Hyman, author of *The Most Expensive Game in Town: The Rising Cost of Youth Sports and the Toll on Today's Families,* he's being realistic. He's not grasping for a coveted NCAA Division I scholarship. "College is hugely competitive. I don't even think about college sports for my children. Pro sports are even less realistic. To experience high school sports is kind of what drives us. Some of the fondest memories of my life are about playing high school sports. We want to put our kids in a position to play. And that won't be easy for them, because the high schools they are going to are the most competitive in sports in the country."

Solution: You might be tempted to say, "This is not me. I'm not doing that. That's way too extreme. I'd never spend the kind of money Mr. Dicari spent." But the fact is that it's increasingly become a part of our cultural expectation that parents spend well beyond budget—beyond what should be spent on a child or young athlete.

We all have to be on guard. Spending is accumulative. It's a good idea to keep a running tab like Mr. Dicari did. By the end of the year you may be surprised at what you've spent.

We like to make our kids happy, but kids often have outsize expectations. They can be like roadsters with no brakes. They'll keep on clamoring for the latest team jersey, and marketers know that. It would seem that professional sports teams don new jerseys every weekend to ensure that our kids and our wallets can never keep up.

The truth is that we all want to raise our children in a spirit of gratitude, not entitlement. What is rare is precious. It's important for our children to understand that it's not within our budgets to buy them everything they want. Whether we are struggling or wealthy, there are limits. That's what budgets are. Otherwise we'll just drive off the family fiscal cliff.

This is a great opportunity for our children to learn the value of money. We can be candid with them: "John, we have to dial back a bit and spread out the spending." If participating on a team or buying equipment is a priority for them, we can tell them that if we focus our spending on sports, other things may have to be sacrificed, like going to movies or taking a vacation.

We hope our kids will learn about hard work and perseverance through sports. They can learn such values before they even step on a field. "We never had money when we were kids," says backcountry snowboarding pioneer Jussi Oksanen, "so I had to work for my dad and work different jobs to be able to go snowboarding. You had to buy your season ticket, and that was all your money gone toward that. So you are already paying a lot more attention to what you're doing because you're the one paying. It's not your parents giving you the opportunities and providing trainers and everything else at such a young age."

We can ask our kids to contribute to their sports expenses. It's an opportunity for them to get creative. Let them figure out how they'll earn the money. When Kim's daughter wanted to play basketball, she walked dogs for two months while bouncing a basketball (the dogs got used to it) to pay half of the $140 registration fee. Having to work toward something can itself be a gift. When we put on the brakes, we give our children the gift of anticipation. If we give them everything, we risk creating entitlement monsters.

Some parents we interviewed organize fund-raisers to raise money for team equipment and trips. That's another great way to involve kids, and also to build team and community ties with bake sales, car washes, raffles, and the like. Parents can also set up informal swap shops where clothing and equipment can be traded and shared.

The bottom line isn't about money, however; it's about expectations. A kid's desires have to be put into a larger context, and this also applies to parents. Whether it's a kid who insists on having a new $150 custom-designed bat each year so he can be like his teammates ("They all have one, Dad. Really!") or parents who insist that their children not "lose out" on experiences they remember having as kids, we are better off making sure we have brakes and know how to use them.

Five Better Ways to Invest in Your Kid's Athletic Future—Locally

Think of the improvements your travel team could make at home if you pooled the money you all spend on long-distance tournament play. If you each spend $2,000, and there are fifteen kids on average per team, that's $30,000 you could spend on:

1. Improving the fields in your community or building additional ones.

2. Investing in hands-on training of volunteer (parent) coaches.

3. Bringing in an athletic development coach to work with your team or league for a few weeks during the off-season.

4. Paying to have an EMT and defibrillators at all games, and CPR training for all coaches.

5. Training coaches to recognize key symptoms of concussions and other head injuries.

What Can I Do About the Erosion of Family Time?

Our kids love playing team sports. We shuttle them from practice to game and back again and just don't seem to have time together as a family anymore. We don't even get to have sit-down meals together. I feel like I'm losing touch. Is this just me not wanting to let go?

Discussion: Not at all. What you are feeling is quite natural. It's exhaustion, or at least weariness. It's nostalgia for something quite legitimate—a moment or hour when your family can bond, when there's no going to or coming from anything. Just being together. *Just being.* Your lifestyle, jam-packed as it is with activities and sports-parenting commitments, has become overwhelming.

We are under so much pressure to stimulate and entertain and engage our kids. We want them to log hours of great experiences, learn new skills, become physically and socially confident and adept. So we insert them in sports programs at the tender age of four or five or six, and once we are on that treadmill, there's no getting off.

Countless parents have told us that they are exhausted, physically and emotionally, by the efforts they make scheduling, driving to, coaching, and/or team managing at youth sporting events. One mother admitted she secretly prays for rain—as her son and daughter lay out their uniforms the night before games in eager anticipation—because that would mean the onslaught of commitments would grind to a halt and the family could share quiet indoor time together.

Solution: Children's involvement in sports should be a pleasure and a privilege. We'd like to make the case for *less is more.* When things get too crazed, cut back. Simplify. You can exchange the gift of participation for the gift of anticipation.

Luis's sons are good soccer players, and they clamored since the age of nine to play on travel teams. They were drawn to the excitement of playing in competitive tournaments against challenging opponents, and, of course, they *really* liked those cool travel uniforms! It was quite tempting to sign them right up, but rather than cave in, Luis assured them that they would get a chance when they were a little older. This built up interest and excitement, and bought time to allow them to hold on to childhood a little longer. There is nothing wrong with delayed gratification, with having something to look forward to, with saying, "not right now."

Scheduling can certainly be a nightmare, but sacrificing family dinners and other bonding experiences like relaxing family vacations (and just about every weekend and most holidays) to participate in practices, games, and tournaments is not the best way to build strong, lasting, healthy family ties. That's why taking a season off can be so beneficial. If you have two or more kids, time it so that they all take the same season off from sports. Then you can provide your family with windows through which to reconnect: activities that include everyone and have no competitive thrust to them. We've said this before, but it's worth saying again: Try simpler things like a family hike, an all-day fishing trip, or an evening spent working together on a 1,000-piece jigsaw puzzle. Such activities are shifts in rhythm that draw families closer and restore balance and flow.

Kim wanted to make sure that his daughters understood all that goes into signing up for multiple afternoon activities, so he had them take out paper and markers and draw up their own detailed schedules. They were instructed to include the time it took to get ready and drive to and from activities. Then the family sat down and reviewed everything to see what was doable and what had to be put off until more life space was available.

Balance, like the perfect hook shot, is elusive. You have to work at it, and often parents have to impose it. We can remind ourselves and our kids to slow down, take a deep breath, and exhale slowly. Everything doesn't have to be done right now. It's important to schedule breaks, real downtime, time for rest and creativity to balance activity. *We can't always be doing. We need to exhale, too. We need quiet time at home, together.*

What if My Kid Is Too Passive?

My kid holds back too much. He's just not aggressive enough and is more of a spectator than a participant. This causes him to perform poorly. How can I get him to step it up?

Discussion: We get it. You don't want your kid to be passive. You want him right in there participating fully. But let's be clear: This is not a question of aggression, but of engagement. Aggressiveness is not a positive—assertiveness is. Every kid has his own doorway into engagement. The last thing you want to do is push your child to become "aggressive" *right now,* if he's prone to be cautious. In the long run, you might well push him straight toward quitting. That's a real concern, and we've seen it happen again and again: Kids quit sports in droves.

It's helpful to take a step back and consider how your child learns things in general, not just in sports. When it comes to math or the language arts, does he need to have a sense of the big picture before he can grapple with the details? What about new social situations? When your son steps into the room at a party, what does he do? Does he hang back a bit and take in the room? Is he a hesitant kid? If so, that's perfectly fine. That's who he is, and that's his temperament. He may be a bit catlike, standing back and watching things unfold while he figures it all out. Then, in his own way and in his own time, he'll enter into the mix. If he's already participating on a team, that's great. It's not as if he's checked out or doesn't want to take part at all. But if he's an introverted type and you push him—"Come on, Joey! You've gotta get in there and tackle harder. Don't just stand there! Go for it. What are you waiting for?"—he may react either by becoming stubborn or withdrawn.

Solution: For kids, sports are more about the relationships they have with the children they play with than performance. Left alone, they are not likely to obsess about making a hard tackle or winning games. So if you want a kid to become more involved, practically, in the sports he plays, focus on developing your child's level of engagement and confidence. Our strategy is to create activities for the child that can socially orient him within the team, away from the field or court. Throw a pizza party or invite teammates over for play dates. If your child is a bit shy, don't invite a large group of kids, just one or two. This will help him find that doorway into taking part in a more wholehearted way.

The fact that your child is not assertive is not at all unusual. Again and again, on teams we coach we encounter kids who are naturally assertive—who rush in there and engage fearlessly in every play or tackle—and kids who are hesitant and seem to stop and give up too easily. Parents get frustrated, but patience is pivotal.

We've found that it can take two or three years for a child to develop positive assertiveness. One nine-year-old whom Luis coached in soccer was unable to engage with his opponents. He'd tackle tentatively and seemingly halfheartedly. Once beaten—which happened pretty much every time—he'd just turn and watch the player who got by him dribble downfield. His parents were clearly frustrated by his lack of tenacity. "He's just not a go-getter," they'd say. "That's the way he is with everything." They seemed resigned.

But the kid did love to play. He never missed a practice, and he stuck with the team for three years. Toward the end of the second year, three things changed: His bond with his teammates strengthened, he became physically stronger, and his skills and coordination improved steadily. As his confidence grew, so did his level of engagement. By the end of the third year he was a completely different player: He won tackles, stole the ball often, and when beaten during one game, immediately reengaged three times with the player who'd dribbled past him.

What forms a foundation here is the dynamic we call "inhabiting your space." A kid does not need to get "into someone's face" or play hard to the point of borderline recklessness in order to be assertive. In fact, this can often be a sign that a player has "lost it" or is "getting out of it." What they are "getting out" of is ownership of their *own* space. Instead they are trying to insert themselves into someone else's space. The impression may be that they are being strong and assertive, but we have seen that this often leads to a drop in performance for the aggressor, who becomes "uncentered."

Instead what we hope to cultivate in a young athlete is the ability to hold, or inhabit, his own space, first by standing strong when challenged, and second by learning to challenge and chase his opponent. Some kids feel this is not okay; it feels like aggression to them. In a way they are right. Try to help your son differentiate between appropriate tackling and defending, and over-the-top aggressiveness. Help him understand that holding and inhabiting his space when challenged or challenging others is part of the game. It's a little like "spatial fencing," in which there will be interplay between two fencers. Each searches for a gap in the other's defense.

A finely tuned athlete is both centered and aware of the activity around him. He has a wonderful sense of timing, of when to go for it and when to hold back. That marks the difference between aggressiveness and assertiveness.

A final thing to bear in mind: Kids often lack assertiveness because they have an underlying fear of failure. That can be at the root of what prompts them to hold back. A parent or coach steeped in the Whole Child Sports ethos, which redefines the way winning and success are measured, realizes that a young player who lacks assertiveness needs time and coaxing. Time and again we have watched children we've trained develop appropriate assertiveness and enjoy the spatial interplay that it involves. All they needed was the time and space to "inhabit their own space."

How Do I Help My Young Athlete Find the Proper Flow in Movement?

My thirteen-year-old daughter is slower than her teammates. She's developed good soccer skills, but she struggles to get around the field quickly. Some of her friends attend speed and agility training classes several times a week. They seem quicker and more coordinated than they were last season. Should I expose my daughter to this type of training at her age? Does it work for everyone?

Discussion: Many people think speed is an innate gift, but the truth is that anyone can get faster. Speed is a skill composed of a series of specific synchronized movements. World-class sprinters spend countless training hours perfecting their running techniques. In martial arts, the more time you spend perfecting your movements, the faster you become at deflecting and delivering kicks and punches. This principle also applies to running.

Solution: Kids who are twelve and older often experience rapid growth spurts, which make them look and feel awkward when they move. This is an ideal time for a young athlete to develop body awareness, running technique, and basic dynamic strength. Proficiency does wonders for self-esteem and overall performance. Once children experience improvements in speed, strength, and stamina, their newly acquired body confidence spills over to all their other sport-specific activities.

When taught basic athletic skills and the correct biomechanics of sport-specific movements by an experienced professional, your son or daughter will improve. Scott has been an athletic performance coach for more than two decades and works with several youth sports organizations that want their players to develop basic movement skills. "If you disregard this vital portion of development training, you are building your child's athletic future on a foundation of sand," he says. "In order to provide your kid with the best opportunity to execute at his or her optimal level, athletic movement training is essential."

What exactly is athletic movement training? It is the development of basic athletic skills such as agility, balance, coordination, speed, strength, and stamina. You may have been led to believe that these skills are honed during regular sport-specific training, and to a certain degree they are, but sport-specific skills are often made up of a collection of multiple complex movements. A young athlete who has not properly learned basic athletic skills will be at a distinct disadvantage when she tries to execute more advanced sport-specific skills. She will also be more prone to injury.

Take a look at ball control in soccer as an example. When a soccer coach introduces a drill to teach the player who has possession of the ball to fend off a defender, he demonstrates specific ball-shielding techniques. What coaches rarely teach are the basic athletic skills necessary to execute these movements: upper and lower body coordination; eye-foot coordination; change of direction; balance; lower and upper body core strength. In essence, he's teaching the youth a technique that requires a compendium of skills that she has not yet developed. Athletic movement skills are essential for pretty much every sports-specific movement or skill.

Over the past several years athletic training schools have popped up across the country. They are the latest fad in the world of sports training. Many personal trainers also provide it. "My suggestion is, proceed with caution," says Scott. "Though I believe in this type of training, not everyone has the skills or training to teach it properly. Coaches from the youth to the high school level may attempt to provide and incorporate athletic movement training into their practices, but, unless they've been trained and certified to do so, the chances are your daughter will not receive proper training."

The following are three athletic movement skill and performance programs that we recommend (ideal for Stage Three: age twelve to fifteen):

1. Parisi Speed Schools

2. Athletes' Performance

3. Velocity Athletic Training

What if My Child Is More Interested in Skateboarding than Team Sports?

My child spends hours fooling around on his skateboard. All he seems to want to do is work on tricks and flips. I'm concerned that his time could be better spent on anything from homework to team sports.

Discussion: Most parents we speak to complain that their kids spend too much time indoors, plugged into a variety of devices like televisions, computers, phones, and video games, so you may want to count your blessings. Your son is out there, engaged, and he's passionate about what he's doing, which is great. Repetition is critical to the development of skill, especially in sports, yet kids often get bored when they have to practice moves or sports drills over and over. They don't like repetition and lose focus quickly. However, your son shows perseverance.

Solution: Our advice: Let him be. He has found an activity—in this case skateboarding—that's challenging and physical, and it will help him develop creativity and problem-solving skills. There are several things he's learning out there on that board. One is how to overcome adversity, and another is how to self-coach. Sports like skateboarding require a great deal of focus. As you try to develop proficiency with tricks, you constantly make mistakes. That can be discouraging, but if your son is out there working hard, he is learning that in order to master a move or trick, you must work through your mistakes. You have to try something, adjust your approach, and perhaps fail again. He's learning experientially and discovering that learning is a process that takes time, and that there's no instant gratification. That's a great sports lesson and a great life lesson, too.

The fact that your son practices for hours on end, mistake after mistake, without giving up, is quite impressive to us. And the payoff is huge. As street trial-bike riding phenom Danny MacAskill explains, "I'll just sort of think of something new and try it . . . it's really just about trying it over and over until you get it. If you pull something big, it's a real feeling of joy and accomplishment."

Action sports are flashy and dynamic, and sometimes the counterculture bad-boy images that marketers cultivate are a bit off-putting to parents. But at the heart of the process of learning sports such as snowboarding, skateboarding, and trial street-bike riding are lessons that organized team sports could benefit from. On a purely athletic level, action sport athletes (and your skateboarding son) are developing balance, agility, and coordination. Such basic athletic skills are critical to success in any sport. What these sports demand is a blend and balance of three essential elements: training, continued learning, and free play—a creative process in which athletes develop multiple moves and tricks in different scenarios while continuously making adjustments and improvements.

These kids meet up at skate parks or on mountaintops and confer, and no matter what their skill level, ability, or age, they coach each other. Everyone is focused on practicing the execution of fundamentals, which will help them succeed. The self-coaching and peer coaching that go on as kids spend not hours, or days, but months, even years, working on and perfecting one technical aspect of a challenging trick is invaluable. Such settings are breeding grounds for creativity. Says superstar snowboarder Jussi Oksanen, "No one snow boarder is the same, and no one trick is the same. That's the beauty of it. You are really getting a feel for how creative you are because the terrain and conditions are changing constantly. And you have to figure things out as you go."

When your son has worked through a move or trick and can execute it perfectly, and even improve upon it, he reaches what's referred to as a state of flow. It's a magical moment in which everything you've worked on clicks. It's a moment of mastery. It's what every athlete, musician, and writer strives for: that split second when practice and passion blend seamlessly and produce peak performance.

In order to make organized youth sports more dynamic, challenging, interesting, and inspiring, it is essential to blend this passionate self-teaching and peer mentoring with effective traditional coaching methods so that young athletes in team sport settings can develop the level of creativity and adaptability that is often achieved in action sports training. University of North Carolina women's lacrosse coach Jenny Levy implements such dynamic training methods in her program (see chapter 4). Whole Child Sports encourages this at all age levels. It's exactly what our children need to prepare them to become well-rounded athletes and capable young adults.

The Proper Balance between Training and Playing

Proper conditioning and preparation is one of the most over-looked aspects of youth sports. Despite the overwhelming emphasis placed on winning, many parents and coaches don't prepare kids properly to compete. The result: subpar perfor-mance, minor injuries that hamper players—often setting the stage for major injuries that curtail their involvement alto-gether—and physical and mental burnout.

Balance and Flow in a Young Athlete's Conditioning Development

According to Jason Gromelski, a New York City–based physi-cal therapist, NATA-certified athletic trainer, and SCA-certified strength and conditioning specialist who has worked with profes-sional and collegiate athletes and dancers for more than a decade, strength and conditioning training can help prevent injuries in younger athletes. These training programs develop the relation-ship between an athlete's nerves and muscles and increase the fluidity of overall movement patterns. Be wary about download-ing college- or professional-level fitness athletic programs and applying them to children or youth athletes. They can do more damage than good. Programs should be customized to match each young athlete's physical and mental maturity, and the train-ing should be varied and fun in order to keep kids engaged.

The following chart clarifies what types of training and conditioning activities are appropriate for the three key stages in a child's physical development: prepubescence, puberty, and postpubescence. Here's how these categories fit within the general Whole Child Sports age and stage sports development guidelines outlined in chapter 1 (keep in mind that individual children develop physically at different rates, and girls generally develop earlier than boys): Stage One (five- to eight-year-olds) coincides with the prepubescent category. Children begin Stage Two (ages nine to eleven) in the prepubescent category but transition into puberty by the end of this stage. Stage Three (ages twelve to fifteen) generally fits within the chart's puberty stage, and in Stage Four (ages sixteen to eighteen) boys and girls are moving from puberty into the postpubescent stage.

	Prepubescent	Puberty	Postpubescent
Cardiovascular training	Active free play	Yes	Yes
Strength training	Active free play	2–3 sets of 6–15 reps using body weight, elastic bands, tubing (no dumbbells)	Free to perform good quality strengthening programs (submaximum to maximum weight loads)
Agility training	Active free play	Yes	Yes
Stretching	Active free play	Yes	Yes
Balance and proprioception	Active free play	Yes	Yes
Power training	No	Begin (not frequent)	Yes

Understanding the terms:

- **Cardiovascular training:** improving stamina

- **Strength training:** doing things like push-ups, pull-ups, and using dumbbells

- **Agility training:** making quick changes of direction; footwork

- **Stretching:** performing dynamic warm-ups and warm-downs
- **Balance and proprioception:** orienting your body in space
- **Power training:** developing explosive movement (e.g., sprinting while being held back)

During the prepubescent stage, emphasis should be placed on helping the child to understand his body and how it moves. This can be called the "Gumby" stage, when the body's connective tissues are beginning to take shape and can adapt very easily to demands but can also be overstretched. Real care needs to be taken during this stage in sports like gymnastics and dance, because some coaches overburden kids, asking too much of this supple stage for the sake of performance. This risks serious damage both now and into adulthood. Functional movement patterns, cardiovascular conditioning, balance, proprioception, and stretching should be the emphasis during this stage.

As the athlete progresses into puberty, the emphasis and intensity of the strength program can increase. In addition, cardiovascular conditioning, agility, balance and proprioception, and a cautious stretching program can be developed.

At around sixteen, the athlete can begin to develop an adult-level workout regimen. The focus of the program should be on strength and power, though such a workout should be balanced with agility, balance, and proprioception training. Rest days should be incorporated into the training program. Light and heavy exercise days should be alternated as well.

The Shocking Injury Statistics in Youth Sports

It's up to us as parents to ensure that our young athletes follow properly balanced preseason and in-season training and conditioning programs in order to proactively prevent injuries. Millions of us are guilty of contributing to the win-at-all-costs mind-set that's dominated the child and youth sports landscape over the past decade, and our children are getting seriously hurt as a result. Let's take a hard look at some startling statistics from StopSportsInjuries.org:

- High school athletes account for an estimated 2 million injuries, 500,000 doctor visits, and 30,000 hospitalizations each year.

- More than 3.5 million kids under age fourteen receive medical treatment for sports injuries each year.

- Children ages five to fourteen account for nearly 40 percent of all sports-related injuries treated in hospitals. On average, the rate and severity of injury increase with a child's age.

- Overuse injuries are responsible for nearly half of all sports injuries to middle and high school students.

- Although 62 percent of organized-sports-related injuries occur during practice, one-third of parents do not have their children take the same safety precautions at practice as they would during a game.

- Twenty percent of children ages eight to twelve and 45 percent of those ages thirteen to fourteen will have arm pain during a single youth baseball season.

- Injuries associated with participation in sports and recreational activities account for 21 percent of all traumatic brain injuries among children in the United States.

- According to the Centers for Disease Control, more than half of all sports injuries in children are preventable.
- Among athletes ages five to fourteen, 28 percent of football players, 25 percent of baseball players, 22 percent of soccer players, 15 percent of basketball players, and 12 percent of softball players were injured while playing their respective sports.
- Since 2000 there has been a fivefold increase in the number of serious shoulder and elbow injuries among youth baseball and softball players.

If we are harboring a secret hope that our son or daughter will become an elite athlete, we should heed this statistical wake-up call: While more than thirty-eight million kids play sports each year, just 2 percent of high school athletes in America will secure a sports scholarship to an NCAA school. And the chances your child-athlete will fulfill your Olympic dreams for them? Well, we all need to keep this in mind: A grand total of 529 athletes competed for the United States at the 2012 Olympics in London.

We want our children to fulfill their athletic potential and become the best they can be, but in pushing them too hard, and in an imbalanced manner, we run the risk of derailing their athletic aspirations. In some cases, it can result in permanent physical disabilities. That's something no parent wants for his or her child.

Injury Prevention
To keep your kid from getting hurt, follow these guidelines:

- Get a preseason evaluation (physical and general strength and conditioning assessment).
- Perform good preseason training.
- Use the proper equipment (e.g., cleat size and type, based on playing surface).
- Eliminate pressures to win.
- Get proper nutrition.
- Get enough rest, relaxation, and sleep.

Warning Signs of Injury

Our young athletes don't always tell us when they're suffering from an injury. They may be too excited about playing, worried about being forced to miss games, or concerned about letting down their teammates. They may also be worried about disappointing us—their parents—because they know, consciously or subconsciously, how vested we are in their success, and how much time and money we've sacrificed to provide them with opportunities to play sports.

Keep an eye out for the following warning signs of injury, keeping in mind that you may notice a combination of several of the symptoms, or just one or two that manifest more severely.

- Withdrawal
- Irritability (personality changes)
- Decreased athletic performance
- Avoidance of participation in sport (e.g., making excuses in order to not attend practice)
- Decreased excitement about practice

- Chronic complaints of joint or muscle pain
- Poor grades

Treat the Off-Season as Exactly That

A Whole Youth athlete balances athletic development with other life activities. Rest and relaxation are an important part of that balance, as are other mental and athletic activities like reading, making music, creating art, hiking, riding a bike, or working odd jobs around the house. Any and all of these activities serve as important developmental counterpoints to athletic training and participation in team sports.

Too many young athletes go from one season to the next without a break: football to basketball; basketball to baseball; soccer to lacrosse. Whatever the combination, there is little or no downtime. In fact, seasons often overlap, with preseason training for one sport starting before another sport's season has ended. In some cases, athletes play the same sport as the seasons change (e.g., fall soccer becomes winter indoor soccer, which morphs into spring soccer and summer soccer camps). Parents and coaches rarely talk about blocking a season out for rest and relaxation.

There is nothing wrong with a team sport athlete taking off an entire season each year to focus on schoolwork or explore other activities, such as individual sports, creative development through writing and art projects, and even simply to hang out with friends more often. An athlete who develops creative skills outside of sports is honing creative awareness, which can also be applied to sports when she returns to team play. It's just like a songwriter or artist who takes a deliberate break from the confines of a project to explore something entirely different and return to her work fresh and reinvigorated. We cannot stress the importance of creative development in athletes enough. It is vital to the overall process (see chapter 4).

Physical Balance

Balance and stability training are key elements of a well-rounded athlete's fitness routine, but they are often overlooked. Some coaches and players don't understand how integral these elements are to athletic development and performance, while others mistakenly believe that they or their players have good balance already. As they see it, you either have good balance or you don't. Balance should be treated like a muscle; you have to develop and strengthen it to operate optimally.

Four different body systems are integral to balance:

1. **The vestibular system.** It sends signals to the neural structures that control eye movements and to the muscles that keep a person upright.

2. **Vision.** It provides the body with orientation in space and helps stabilize us in relation to the ground and objects around us.

3. **Proprioceptors.** These are sensory receptors on nerve endings found in muscles, tendons, joints, and the inner ear. Proprioception has been called the "sixth sense." It's basically a mechanism—or, more accurately, a series of mechanisms—that keeps track of and controls muscle tension and movement in the body. The receptors relay information about motion or position and make us aware of our own body position and movement in space.

4. **The core (hip and trunk muscle groups).** This is composed of as many as thirty-five different muscle groups connecting into the pelvis from the spine and hip area. To better understand the core muscles, divide them into four regions: back extensors, abdominals, lateral trunk muscles, and hip muscles. The core is the center of gravity; it's where all movement begins. It's also the center of stability for the lower limbs, from the foot to the hip. In order for muscles to move bone, other muscles need to hold onto bones, creating a solid base. The core muscles function as stabilizers and/or bone mobilizers. Core strengthening has a direct positive effect on rotational power, change of direction, jumping, speed, body leverage, and proper posture, all of which are vital to athletic performance.

How to Develop Balance and Stability in a Young Athlete

While working as a professional athletic performance coach, Scott discovered that most athletes and fitness enthusiasts know very little about balance training. Even some elite athletes struggle to perform basic balance drills, like holding one foot off the ground at different heights for an extended period of time, and have poor posture, which affects an athlete's center of gravity and stability. Paying attention to balance and stability will help improve athletic performance and reduce the likelihood of injury.

So if balance is so important, how can parents and coaches incorporate balance training into their children's lifestyles? To entice kids to engage in balance and stability training, we must make it fun and challenging—but not too challenging. The last thing you want is for a young athlete to become frustrated and give up because the bar has been set too high, too early. The following are four ways to develop balance and stability.

1. **Train with a Vew-Do NUB Board.** This balance board can be used by athletes from youth to elite levels. It incorporates dynamic movements: The board can be walked both forward and backward; it can be maneuvered through obstacle courses; you can perform 360-degree rotations.

   The benefits are multiple and far-reaching. With consistent practice, a young athlete can develop dynamic balance, body awareness, core strength, and better range of motion, all of which increase muscle stability and rotational power, and help prevent foot, ankle, knee, hip, and lower back injuries.

   While the board is frequently used by professional snowboarders, soccer players, and golfers, among others, it's great for kids as well because it sits fractions of inches off the ground and is not intimidating. With consistent practice, individuals can learn quickly and get better every time they use the board. Most important, it's fun.

2. **Vary the young athlete's balance training experience.** Training in a gym can get tedious, so instead introduce activities that are balance focused but also a lot of fun: Sports like mountain biking, skiing, ice skating, snowboarding, and climbing are great cross-training options. Kids develop balance and stability while having fun and learning a new activity.

3. **Build balance training into team practice routines.**
   If you want to grab your team's attention, mix up the
   rhythm of your practice, and develop their balance and
   stability, by introducing them to a balance obstacle
   course. Visit www.wholechildsports.com to see one
   specially developed for high school basketball practices.

4. **Build a basic balance obstacle course in your
   backyard or park.** Whether children walk, jump, or
   jog through them, obstacle courses are challenging
   and fun, and help kids develop balance, agility,
   coordination, and body strength (see "Backyard /
   Local Park Obstacle Course" in chapter 6).

The Ten Tenets of a Balanced Whole Youth Sports Experience

Consider these ten principles to provide an ideal balance of
active and educational play and foster a healthy mix of mental
and physical development in your young athlete each year.

1. **Play one sport per season.** When a kid plays more
   than one sport, she often ends up with little free
   time. Kids need downtime to exhale, regroup, and
   recharge emotionally. They also need to rest and
   recover physically from training, and, of course,
   they need time to properly focus on schoolwork.
   Furthermore, a cluttered athletic schedule impinges
   on all-important family time, essential to the
   development of healthy, supportive family ties. The
   bottom line: A kid should be able to fully enjoy one

particular sport rather than be overcommitted and harried. Fun, not frenzy, is the key.

2. **Play different sports during different seasons.** Avoid specialization at an early age, or at any age, for that matter; it is problematic both physically and mentally. Kids need a variety of athletic experiences to develop better motor skills and limit burnout. Playing different sports also helps prevent wear-and-tear injuries (seen surprisingly frequently nowadays in children as young as nine or ten) and, most importantly, keeps them passionate about playing well into adolescence and beyond. Forcing kids to develop one sport at the expense of others can turn training into a grind and playing into a perpetual performance review, rather than what it should be: fun and invigorating.

3. **Play competitive sports a maximum of three seasons per year.** Take one or two seasons off to discover and explore other activities that are challenging, but not necessarily team oriented. This expands an athlete's skill set and broadens his perspective. After consecutive seasons of soccer, basketball, and lacrosse, for example, the stress of competition can wear on a youth. Relaxing or trying something different like surfing, kayaking, hiking, or even fishing is a great way to learn, achieve balance, and rest mind and body for next year's athletic endeavors.

4. **Engage in at least one activity per year that involves the development and mastery of balance.** Balance

is an often overlooked, yet vital, cornerstone of athletic development. Most sports require young athletes to find or maintain balance during the flow of competition while attempting to execute other actions, such as making a hockey slap shot, completing a golf shot, rebounding a basketball, or completing an infield play. Work on improving balance helps a child develop core strength and rotational force, which is vital for optimal performance in sports. Incorporating a balancing activity that is both fun and challenging (like skateboarding, mountain biking, skiing, or snowboarding) is a great way to improve a young athlete's capabilities in a favorite team sport.

5. **Study the history of the sports you play.** Kids should not miss the opportunity to get to know the colorful background of their favorite sports. Learning about how, when, and where the sport was invented and how it has evolved will give them a great historical perspective and deeper appreciation for the sport.

6. **Learn all the rules of your sports.** Many athletes have found that a thorough knowledge of rules of the sport they play deepens their understanding and can give them a distinct competitive advantage. For example, even at the elite professional level, PGA golfers have learned the hard way what can happen when you make decisions midtournament without a proper grasp of the rules. Such errors have cost them strokes and thousands if not hundreds of thousands of dollars.

Raymond Berry, retired NFL New England Patriots head football coach, was famous for quizzing his players and carefully reviewing the rules with them at least once a week. Berry believed that with a thorough, frequently refreshed grasp of the rules, his players would have a better understanding of how the game is played and therefore make fewer mental mistakes and have a distinct advantage over their opponents.

7. **Arrange for your young athlete to help coach.** If you've ever had to teach, you understand the amount of preparation that goes into doing a good job. Teaching also provides you with a great learning experience. The very fact that you are required to explain something to someone else forces you to think through the entire process and understand it much more clearly. Providing a young athlete with the opportunity to coach (or assistant coach) a younger child or team is a great training experience for him or her: Learning through teaching can translate directly into deeper understanding and improved performance on the field.

8. **Provide practices that challenge and engage the kids.** This suggestion applies to both parents in their backyards and youth sports coaches. We often hear that kids don't want to attend practice or learn a new skill, complaining that practice is boring, it's not fun, and the kids aren't seeing any improvement in their own skills. Many youth sports coaches have little time to prepare, or they lack the knowledge to run

a practice that teaches the fundamentals but is also dynamic enough to engage every kid. Practices often devolve into scrimmages, where coaches teach very little and groups of kids are forced to sit, watch, and wait. Whether you are at home or at a team practice, you should do your homework, consult the experts, and set up a circuit to engage and challenge kids as you teach them fundamentals and technique. Kids should be rotated frequently between drill stations to keep them physically active and mentally engaged. Parents and coaches should make sure to spend as little time as possible explaining things verbally to players. It's better to show them what you want them to learn. If you do need to talk with them, engage them in conversation rather than lecture them. Elicit observations from your kid or the team. They will surprise you with their acute insights on what they are doing well and what they need to focus on more to improve.

9. **Teach kids how their bodies work.** The best way to get youth athletes to understand why you're doing a particular exercise is to educate them on how the body works, including what muscles and joints are involved in sports activities and why it's important that they be developed to increase strength and avoid injury. Introducing your youth athlete to the body's anatomy is an important first step in understanding how the body works (for book or DVD recommendations visit www.wholechildsports.com).

10. **Train the brain: build / create / problem-solve.**
    An important, often overlooked element of athletic
    development is cognitive development. When kids
    play in their backyards or at the park with friends,
    making up games, building tree forts, or designing
    obstacle courses, they are actively learning how to
    think and problem-solve. When engaged in novel
    tasks, they have to learn to make adjustments and
    work out solutions. In organized sports, kids are often
    given too much instruction before, during, and after
    games, and are not allowed to figure things out for
    themselves. Coaches bark orders about playing in
    position rather than allowing kids to learn from their
    mistakes and adjust on the fly. Challenge your kids
    at home, and then find a coach who does the same
    on the field. Start by setting up areas in your house
    for creative play and experimentation (see chapter
    6). Introduce new things they can build in the living
    room or backyard. Change their environment: Take
    your kid for an exploration hike or bike ride. These
    varied experiences help them develop creativity
    and adaptivity, critical building blocks of cognitive
    development that will complement their physical and
    emotional growth.

CHAPTER 8

Beyond Winning—
A New Paradigm for Youth Sports Competition

In this final chapter, we set forth our picture of a new system for youth sports development. Each of us has tested different elements over the years we have coached, yet we all have children who have participated in some form of the traditional system. Scott's son, who loves baseball and basketball, has played on two travel teams. Kim's daughters have played ultimate Frisbee and basketball and run track. Luis's daughter played high school volleyball and basketball, and his three younger sons played on recreational soccer teams. All our kids have loved participating and had a lot of fun with their friends.

In this chapter we change gears a bit. You'll find a blueprint that, while it appears to be aimed at coaches, is included to give you, the parent, an overview of how Whole Youth Sports works. Once you have that, you can see how your kid's program, or the one he's going into, measures up. You will be armed with practical alternatives that make sense and confirm that hunch you've had all along—the feeling that "I knew that, and now I can express it in a sensible and informed way." It's important because parents are often called upon to coach or assistant coach in youth sports, and if that's not you, it may be someone you know and *can influence.*

We hope you take portions of what we present here and test them out, providing your kid, league, or community with small doses of this new approach. Perhaps you can start your preseason several weeks early and incorporate some of the developmental methods outlined in this chapter. During the off-season, form a discussion group with as many moms and dads as you can gather. Start conversations, seek feedback, and share your stories with us at WholeChildSports.com. In whatever form it takes, keep the conversation going. The best way to make practical changes is to engage as many people as you can.

As we write about changing the way youth sports are taught and experienced, we recognize that it's not necessarily simple to implement the changes and solutions we recommend and launch a new approach in your community. We've all witnessed and read about the many difficulties and ills that affect organized youth sports. That's why the three of us have come together to offer you suggestions to guide you and your children through this winding, occasionally treacherous, journey. If even one drill we recommend, one game, one list, one answered question, or even an entire chapter inspires you to improve your kid's sports experience, we will consider our efforts a success. At the end of the day, all that matters is that you help your child and the kids around him or her.

Too much of today's youth sports system is predicated on signing up as many kids as possible and rushing them onto "elite," "premier," or "travel" teams, so that they can "make" their high school team and "earn" a college scholarship. Yet only 2 percent of high school athletes are awarded scholarships each year. We believe that youth sports consumes too large a share of precious family time, and that scores, wins, and championships should not stand out as the definitive measures of success. We feel your frustration and share your concerns.

Youth organizations are unfortunately notorious battlegrounds for politicking and township infighting. Dozens of parents we interviewed described simmering arguments and, in some cases, major tensions between board members, administrators, coaches, and parents in organizations that purport to be unwaveringly focused on promoting "fun, fair play, and fundamentals." Often an Old Guard resists things like rule changes or league restructuring and locks horns with a breakaway faction that presses for change.

The progress that John Gualtiere and his friends have made in a conservative, hypercompetitive town like Ossining, New York, in a sport as red, white, and blue as football, should motivate us all. For Gualtiere the catalyst for change was an incident he witnessed on the football field in 2008, the day of his son Rudy's christening. "I remember every detail, because it was such an important day for us, and my wife kept calling to make sure I wasn't going to be late for church."

Gualtiere was coaching an Ossining flag football team in a game against another town's squad. "In the middle of the game the other team's coach rips into a six-year-old for missing a block. It was absolutely absurd. And the kid was crying. I went up to this coach, this father, my peer, and said, in a quiet voice off to the side so that only he could hear me, 'Are you kidding me? Yelling at this kid like that about a block? I mean, what the hell is wrong with you?' His response shocked me even more. 'You have no idea what this is about. If you want to give your kids lollipops and candy canes over there in Ossining, that's your deal. Because we're here to teach football!'"

Soon after, Gualtiere became the commissioner of the flag football league, and after building up its enrollment to one hundred kids, he pulled Ossining out of the regional league and formed a local teams-only organization. "I wanted to make sure we'd never have to travel again and deal with that. Young kids shouldn't have to witness that kind of thing."

In 2012 Gualtiere became president of Ossining Little League Football, which oversees the flag football league along with the tackle divisions for older kids. With his friends on the league board, he set about making more changes. "We realized we had to come up with a system, a plan to raise the standards of the league." But change does not come easily. "Parents can be ultracompetitive," says Gualtiere. "It's absurd. And they are not always all that easy to deal with. It helps if all the coaches are on board." The idea was to bring in outside expertise, to raise the bar by training a pool of parent-coaches in the fundamentals of football and in coaching techniques. Once the coaches were more effective, they could focus on ensuring that the kids were both learning and having fun. "But we realized we had to win the coaches over first," says Gualtiere. "That wasn't easy. We're a bunch of guys who all played high school football and coached a lot of sports. Some are former NCAA Division I athletes, too. We all have our opinions. 'You gotta do it this way or that way.'"

A friend and former Fordham University varsity basketball teammate told Gualtiere about Scott, who was working at the Parisi Speed School in Jefferson Valley, New York, and developing ideas for the Whole Child Sports program. Scott met with the board and discussed five changes that could be implemented to make Ossining Little League Football a more wholesome program:

1. Focus on developing fundamental skills throughout the August preseason.

2. Provide extensive hands-on coach training, including how to teach fundamental skills, organize a season of practices, and establish realistic team goals related to skill development.

3. Teach each athlete multiple positions.

4. Incorporate fun, nontraditional games in every practice.

5. Include a broad range of athletic and movement training (e.g., agility, balance, speed).

Gualtiere says that after Scott finished his presentation and left, the room went silent. "We all just stared at each other, guys who had played football and coached for years. I don't know about everyone else, but I was thinking to myself, 'We are screwing up our kids. We haven't been teaching them properly from day one.'" The board unanimously approved the recommendations, and Scott spent three weeks working with the league during their 2012 preseason training.

Coaches and kids trained side by side. Rob Healy, father to Aidan and Owen, was impressed. "They learned so much," he said. "The proper way to sprint. How to get off the line. Last year Owen looked like he was stuck in the mud, and this year he was firing out. He had his feet under him. He knew where he was going, and he was accelerating."

More important, the kids had fun. "My son was so excited that each night he laid out his gear for practice the next day," said Steven Packer. "And he walked around the bedroom with his mouth guard on."

They particularly enjoyed the games Scott introduced into practice, though their novelty caught the adults by surprise. "When Scott introduced this Frisbee game in a preseason conditioning practice," says Gualtiere, "everyone wondered, what the h— is he doing? Then it dawned on us. He's making it fun for kids. And isn't that what it's all about?"

At the league's awards assembly, held at Pace University in Pleasantville, New York, in November 2012, two hundred happy little footballers raced up and down the aisles, cutting and weaving through tables packed with adoring parents and friends. As he looked across the hardwood floor at the four hundred guests gathered before him, Gualtiere reflected on the experiences these kids, parents, and coaches had shared throughout the season. He used the word *fun* twenty times over the course of five minutes.

It was the most important message Scott had conveyed: Coaches and parents have to de-emphasize the importance of outcomes. Touchdowns, final scores, and wins don't really matter that much. Having fun is what's paramount. It's something league administrators and coaches across America will say matters most, but that's often just mouthing words. Actions are what speak volumes. This is a mantra Gualtiere and his crew of coaches have fully embraced.

"I'm not gonna kid you," he said. "Sometimes we have to remind each other. We're all human. But we are definitely drinking the Kool-Aid now. We are training these kids to become better athletes, not better football players. Most will never play football past the fifth or sixth grade. That's fine. We just want to make sure that while they were here, playing, they learned a whole lot and had so much fun."

At the end of the night, John summed it up: "Ossining Little League Football has come a long way. But I'll be the first to admit, we've still got a long way to go."

A New Paradigm for Youth Sports Competition

The following are the cornerstones of the Whole Youth Sports program.

Training geared toward the development of the seven key athletic elements: (1) agility, (2) balance, (3) coordination, (4) flexibility, (5) speed, (6) strength, and (7) stamina.

This might seem obvious, and just about every coach in the world would agree that this list "sounds great"; however, in our experience there is too much specialization and overtraining in youth sports. So many kids develop only two or three of these skills, while the others are pretty much neglected.

Total athletic preparedness. You'll hear this term a lot. It means the age-appropriate process of developing a wide range of fundamental skills that can be applied to any sport. As you get older you apply them to your sport of interest, but the key point is that you start broad when you are about twelve and narrow it down as you approach eighteen.

This might sound obvious, and, again, few coaches would disagree. We can picture some of them nodding distractedly. But the reality is that younger and younger children and youths are being streamlined too early into hyperspecialization.

Developing a youth's self-coaching skills. Some of the best learning, which really sinks in deep, happens when kids are given the space to either work alone or get together and self-teach and mentor each other through trial and error, as well as a whole bunch of laughter and friendship.

Coach education and training. We all hope that the people who help shape kids' lives so much know what they are doing and are well trained, but that is not always the case. What we are building here is an ethos that values and develops the Whole Youth: socially, emotionally, and physically. We offer practical ways to take this hope and put it into practice.

You may well ask, if this is "a new paradigm for youth sports competition," where is the competition? Traditional youth sports programs focus on league-structured competitions, with standings that track each team's relative success. The aim of the Whole Youth Sports program is to develop each individual athlete. Competition is woven throughout the entire program, in every session. Kids compete against themselves and each other as they develop individual athletic and sports-specific skills. The final goal is not to win a team championship at the end of each season but to move closer to total athletic preparedness (a.k.a., Whole Youth Sports).

A Whole Youth Sports Training Session Blueprint

The training and practice methods and alternative scorecards presented here are applicable to any sport. Have a quick look at this list, and then see the descriptions that follow.

- Start every session with a ten-minute dynamic warm-up.

- Spend twenty minutes on athletic skill development (one day the focus can be on agility and balance; another on coordination and speed, and so on).

- Have every athlete learn and train for every position.

- Incorporate small-space training and competitions using play and games in every practice session.

- Incorporate self-measuring individual and small-group skill competitions consistently throughout the program.

- Reconfigure the season using a progression toward team competition.

- Set an overarching theme for your season and build toward it with specific goals developed at each practice.

The Ten-Minute Dynamic Warm-Up

Most youth teams and programs begin practice or pregame preparation by simply completing warm-up routines that include anything from static stretching (bending to touch your toes; hurdler stretches) and layup lines (basketball) to playing catch (baseball) and shooting on goal (ice hockey and soccer). A proper warm-up should be much more dynamic and well-rounded than this.

Just as you must warm up a car on a cold winter morning, you should carefully and intentionally warm up your physical vehicle. Proper warm-ups should lubricate all the joints in your body, fire up your nervous system, increase your core body temperature and heart rate, and slowly prepare your cardiovascular system to perform at game speed.

How often have you seen teams start a game playing sluggishly and appearing flat and uninspired? Fatigue or lack of effort is a typical explanation for slow starts, but, in fact, incorrect warm-up routines are often the culprit. Static stretching does not warm up the body and can pave the way to injury rather than prevent it. Attempting to stretch a muscle that has not been properly warmed up first does little to enhance performance.

The key to warm-ups is to keep every athlete moving, utilizing multiple body movements that increase blood flow to all body parts. A basic warm-up that includes the following exercises is much more effective than static stretching or traditional sport-specific drills like layup lines:

- **Squats.** Do proper squats using correct body positioning (shoulders pinched back, head up, chest out, drop to a sitting position with knees just over the toes, weight back on the heels). Complete ten reps three times.
- **Jumping jacks.** Lock arms at the elbows, extended above the head and back to the sides. Jump on the balls of the feet, with shoulders back. Complete ten reps three times.
- **Hand walk.** Walk hands out to push-up position, followed by walking feet to hands. Complete ten yards up and back.
- **Ankle jumps.** Jump up on the balls of the feet quickly; lock knees. Complete twenty reps two times.
- **Knee-to-chest jumps.** Jumps should be consecutive. Complete ten reps two times.

Follow up with these movement drills:

- **Twenty-yard skip.**
- **Twenty-yard shuffle.** Do not cross feet.

- **Forward walking lunges.** Step forward with right leg, lifting your thigh high off the ground. Extend the left leg back straight without the knee touching the ground. Immediately follow that by driving the left thigh up and right leg back without your knee touching the ground. Be sure that the forward knee does not pass over the toes; the back should be straight, shoulders back, and chest out. Each time you land, the heel hits first. Complete twenty yards up and back.

- **Twenty-yard lateral lunges.** The lateral, or side, lunge involves stepping sideways rather than forward. Step sideways to your right two to three feet with your right leg and turn your foot outward at least forty-five degrees. Keep your left foot in place, but allow the outside of your foot to come off the floor. Squat until your right thigh is parallel to the floor. Continue sideways, then switch directions and return to your starting spot.

- **Twenty-yard side run / turn and repeat.** Keep hips square, drive leg over knee, and do not cross feet.

- **Twenty-yard buildup sprints.** Complete four times.

Twenty Minutes of Athletic Skill Development

Select a pair of skills, such as agility and balance, and conduct twenty minutes of fun, fast-paced drills that should be set up in stations prior to the start of practice. The agility station can consist of a combination of agility ladders, small hurdles (six- to twelve-inch banana hurdles), and cones. The balance station can simply be a space that includes a painted or chalked side-line / goal line / hash marks / baseline or a piece of rope laid flat on the ground, and a tennis ball / football.

Conduct one skill at a time over ten continuous minutes by presenting a series of different challenges at each station. Depending on the size of your team, you can split the team into groups that go through multiple stations.

You can select from an evolving series of athletic skill drills for any sport at WholeChildSports.com.

Every Athlete Learns and Trains for Every Position

Coaches have a difficult time following through with this concept. So many of them rush to pigeonhole kids during the first practice of the year in order to set their rosters or fill team positions. That's one key reason we propose this structural redesign of youth sports. So many kids are labeled as a lineman or center in football, a defender in soccer, or a right fielder in baseball when they are too young, and their bodies and skill sets are still evolving. If they are lucky, a well-rounded, knowledgeable coach will put an end to that. Unfortunately, kids sometimes quit a sport altogether because either they have been relegated to a position they have no interest in playing or have a sense that being stuck doing just one thing is "no fun."

When Scott worked for the National Football League, he cocreated the Junior Player Development program, which serves as a model for the total redesign of youth sports training that we propose in this chapter. One of the main tenets of the program was that every kid, no matter his size or ability, be introduced to and taught every position on the football field. It was the fairest, most effective way to prepare kids to play the game and allowed them to experience and figure out what position worked best for them at the moment, and what skills they needed to develop in order to play any other position they liked. Not once was a coach allowed to dictate a position for a particular player.

The results were astounding. "We trained more than 200,000 athletes between the ages of twelve and fourteen who had never played football before," says Scott. "More than 85 percent stuck with the program—which included forty-eight hours of program sessions—to the very end. The kids loved learning this way, and, though it was not our intention to develop pro athletes, several of the kids who participated in the program eventually became NFL players."

This all may sound intriguing, but it's not easy to execute. Every parent-volunteer coach has to be committed to learning the fundamental facets of every position and be able to present and teach them in a manner that captures a young athlete's attention. We offer programs tailored to teaching each sport's fundamental skills on www.wholechildsports.com. Youth leagues and clubs can also hire professionals to implement the program (athletic development experts and sport-specific skill instructors). They can teach your kids and, more importantly, train your coaches so they can implement the program.

Incorporate Small-Space Training and Competitions Using Play and Games in Every Practice Session

We have devoted chapter 4 to laying out the developmental benefits of free play and semistructured play for young athletes. Play and games can also become an important element of structured practices and training sessions. Fundamental skills are vital to athletic development, but when taught in a tedious manner and practiced repeatedly in the same series of drills, they can become tiresome and counterproductive. We recommend that skill-building drills and conditioning be imbedded in dynamic games that kids enjoy playing. That way they are learning and having fun at the same time.

Football

One game that Scott incorporated into his youth football practices became the most popular activity of the entire season: He concluded every practice with a game of Ultimate Football. It's appropriate for all four age stages of the Whole Child Sports developmental continuum (ages five to eighteen). The team was divided into several groups so that games could be run simultaneously. Ultimate Football is similar to Ultimate Frisbee, but you substitute a football for the Frisbee. The object of the game is to score touchdowns in a traditional end zone, but the method is quite different. Rather than being stop-start like football, play is continuous. There are no huddles or downs. Players race up and down the field as they would in Ultimate Frisbee or soccer and can pass the football in any direction. The benefits: Kids get many more touchdowns, they learn to move into open spaces, and they develop great teamwork skills.

When playing the game, these young athletes were unknowingly developing a combination of sport-specific and athletic movement skills. Additionally, they were working on conditioning, because Ultimate Football is a nonstop, free-flow game in which players repeatedly catch, run with, and throw the football (a much better—and more entertaining—way to develop stamina than running laps and windmills). As they passed the football around or defended against their opponents' advances, players were forced to learn team strategy (problem solving and strategizing) without help from coaches, who were not permitted to provide instruction during the game.

Red Zone was another game Scott incorporated into practices so that everyone could enjoy the most exciting elements of football (throwing, catching, and running with the ball) while simultaneously developing skills and physical conditioning. It's great for kids in Stages Two to Four (ages nine to eighteen). Twenty-four players were divided into eight teams of three and set up on four different small-sided fields (twenty yards long by fifteen yards wide). They played three-on-two games (a running clock with two-minute halves) with three players on offense, two on defense, and a sixth player rotating in on defense every play. Offense would switch to defense after each two-minute half ended.

The object of Red Zone is to score as many touchdowns in two minutes as possible, starting with the ball twenty yards from the end zone. Teams that are stopped before reaching the end zone start the next play from where they were stopped, which becomes the new line of scrimmage. When a team scores, they immediately begin again from twenty yards out. With one hand touch, dropped balls, or balls thrown out-of-bounds, play is stopped, and the offense restarts from the original line of scrimmage at the twenty-yard line. Quarterbacks are not permitted to run the ball. Teams are rotated every four minutes until everyone has played each other. At that point, the number of touchdowns scored over the course of all the games by each team is tallied to determine the winning team.

Baseball

In baseball, batting practice can be tedious and frustrating. Typically you see one kid at the plate taking his cuts and fifteen teammates standing around the field, mitts on hips, hoping to shag a ball. What you can do instead to engage everyone is split them into pairs and play Home Run Derby, a game suitable for kids in Stages Three and Four (twelve- to eighteen-year-olds). Purchase 200 short-light golf balls and distribute the balls equally between the pairs of players. Position a player from each pair in the outfield at a predetermined distance from the fence. One player pitches twenty or more consecutive small balls to his partner, who attempts to hit them over the outfield fence. Each batter receives five points for making contact, ten points for hitting the fence, and twenty points for hitting balls over the fence. The players switch roles several times. After a predetermined number of at-bats, each player's points are tallied.

Basketball

One game that helps develop defensive movements and improve reaction time and speed getting downcourt involves mini-Frisbees. It's best suited for Stages Two to Four (ages nine to eighteen). Players line up on the baseline of a basketball court, one at a time, and slide back and forth between two cones placed on the baseline, about ten to fifteen feet apart. The players have their backs to the court. As they slide back and forth, they touch each cone with their outside hand, crouching low in a defensive position. The coach stands behind the players, who are facing the court. He tosses a Frisbee downcourt, and each player must then sprint and chase the Frisbee down before it hits the hardwood. The number of catches made successfully downcourt are counted.

Scott inserted this game midway through a basketball practice Kim and Luis attended in the fall of 2011. The kids had been doing passing drills and were losing steam, but when they started playing the game, they instantly perked up. Within seconds they were laughing, wheezing, and shouting. After the game was over, they returned to their normal practice drills reenergized and excited. Such seemingly unrelated games, used in sport-specific training, can do wonders for the collective mood and energy level of a team, as well as for its skill development.

Back Space is a game Kim played often with the basketball team he coached. It is ideal for youth athletes in Stages Three and Four (ages twelve to eighteen). Kids are restricted to passing the ball behind themselves or to either side. No regular forward passes are allowed. It's a lot of fun but also serves to help develop and strengthen peripheral vision and general awareness. Another game he had them play was Target Ball, which has two scoring systems (also for Stages Three and Four). If a shot hits the large square on the backboard, the shooting team is awarded one point. A shot that hits the smaller square gets two points. Hitting the rim gets you three points, and making a basket counts for four. Players who need encouragement to shoot are awarded "doubler" status. This means that any points they make are doubled when tallied. Thus players who lack the confidence to shoot, and who would normally hand the ball off to "better" players, are motivated to shoot and start to gain confidence as they do. Needless to say, this should be handled with sensitivity, but over many years of playing Target Ball, Kim has never seen a youth overcome by embarrassment upon being conferred "doubler" status. In fact, kids often clamor to be designated the team "doubler."

Volleyball

Anyone who has played or coached volleyball understands the coaching adage, "It's all about moving your feet." Yet many young volleyballers focus on hand-and-arm setting and digging skills, and forget about the footwork required to get them into position to make digging and bumping easy. Blind Prisoner (or Air Raider) is a fun game that develops the lateral foot-movement skills that are the foundation of volleyball success. This game is great for kids in Stages Two to Four (nine to eighteen).

Pin some old blankets to the net on a regulation-size volleyball court (indoor, beach, or grass)—or even to a rope pulled tight across the area if you don't have an available net. Make sure that teams on either side of the blanket cannot see each other. The team that throws the volleyball over the net aims to have it hit the ground on the other side. The team on the receiving end tries to keep the ball from hitting the ground on their side by catching it. Setting, digging, and bumping volleyball skills do not apply. Just good ol' fashioned throwing and catching. If the ball is caught, it gets thrown back to the other side right away. The rally goes on until one of the teams either drops the ball or it hits the ground. If the ball hits the ground or is dropped, the throwing team scores a point.

This game helps players develop great footwork and reflexes. An added benefit: No single player can dominate the game, as can often happen in youth volleyball. For more details and other options (like the semicontrolled chaos of introducing two balls at once in Blind Prisoner), see Kim's book *Games Children Play.*

Incorporate Self-Measuring Individual and Small-Group Skill Competitions Consistently Throughout the Program

We are not proposing that winning a game, league, or championship has no merit and should no longer be the focus of youth sports. However, the single-minded concentration on winning games and reaching the top of league standings is harmful to athletic development. Measuring individual and team progress is a vital part of athletic development, and that is why Whole Youth Sports incorporates individual and small-group competitions in training sessions. Playing such games helps keep athletes focused on their individual goals and breaks up the monotony of skill-based training. It also helps athletes and coaches to monitor their training routines and identify what skills they need to work on.

We have already provided examples of small-group, dynamic, skill-building competitions. Individual skill competitions are equally important and can be tailored to every fundamental that you teach. Every athlete is built differently and possesses different physical abilities and skills at different stages in his or her development. Athletes are not robots and cannot execute skills with textbook perfection. Even professional athletes perform skills in their own personal way. The key is to teach an athlete the basics of a fundamental skill and allow her to adapt it to her own physical ability as she develops it through repeated experimentation. Entertaining individual competitions will help accomplish this and counter the boredom that comes with developing a specific skill through countless repetitions. Kids rise to and enjoy the challenge.

Have you ever noticed how kids perk up when someone takes out a stopwatch, or asks them how high or far they can jump? They immediately want to sprint or jump and quantify their efforts (and yes, this can be used to get children ready for bed on time). We are not talking about pitting one child against another, although they will clamor for that, too. The key is to explain to them that each player is measuring personal progress against his own benchmarks.

The trick here is to establish a young athlete's baseline score for every skill by measuring his performance six to twelve times and then averaging the scores. Once you've established the baseline, you can develop a point system and award points when a player exceeds his base score. This provides him with a way of monitoring his improvement in specific skill areas that the competition is testing. It is particularly helpful when you have players of varying skill levels on a team. The less-skilled athletes now have a concrete way to measure their improvement. As they get better, they become more confident, and a cycle of success is set in motion. Alternatively, if they are measuring themselves only against more experienced and skilled teammates, they will become discouraged.

Reconfigure the Season Using a Progression toward Team Competition

As an athlete reaches the threshold age of twelve (Stage Three), we have found it important to add some traditional gamelike experiences to the other training elements we've already outlined. Ideally, a season can be configured like this:

1. A team trains for a month.

2. The team then competes for several weeks in a traditional league framework. Throughout the competition, individual and team skill progress is carefully measured and emphasized above final scores and placement in standings.

3. Each team can then revert to training for the remaining weeks of the season, retreating to fundamental skill training for a period of time.

For twelve- to fifteen-year-olds, we recommend structuring a season as follows:

- A four-week fundamental skill and conditioning series
- A six-game season
- A second two-week skill and conditioning
- A final six-game season

At the very least, rather than participate in back-to-back seasons of traditional game play, instead break a season into segments that include athletic and skill development segments, or alternate seasons of development with seasons of traditional league play. If training sessions are dynamic and engaging, the kids will not miss full-side games. The parents may wonder where they have gone and even push for them, because they are used to this format or maybe even unconsciously want to be entertained. But really, kids aren't supposed to play for the entertainment of their parents.

Off-season should be just that: Take a break and do not play your main sport for at least three full months. You can try another sport that complements the athletic and sports-specific skills you've been working on, but it's important that it be a sport that does not stress the body in a similar way. For example, a baseball player can switch to basketball or soccer, but you may want to think twice before putting a pitcher in tennis, as the muscle sets, while not identical, are similar enough to hit the pause button. However, a soccer player can benefit from playing tennis or basketball. When you play a sport that requires different skill and movement patterns, you are giving your body a break from the movements it's been conditioned to perform and are simultaneously developing new skill sets that ultimately help you play better in both sports.

Measuring Games beyond the Scoreboard

Even individual traditional games can be measured differently. The following is a sample team scorecard for a soccer match.

TEAM
Sample objectives:

- Create more cross-field movement of ball on offense.

- Create more offensive attacks by moving ball down the wings on defense end of field.

- Prevent counterattacks by regaining possession of ball on offense end of field.

- Maintain possession of ball during midfield transitions.

Sample scoring:
1 point rewarded for every possession moved successfully across the field
1 point for every ball moved down the wings on defense
2 points for every possession regained on offense end of field
2 points for every offensive situation created from midfield
1 point for defensive takeaways in the midfield

INDIVIDUAL
Sample scoring:
2 points for every successful cross-field pass on offensive end of field
1 point for every direct touch off corner kick
1 point for every maintained possession down the wing
2 points for takeaways after loss of possession on offense end of field
1 point for midfield takeaways
2 points for defensive takeaways and successful pass upfield on the wings

Set an Overarching Theme for Your Season and Build toward It with Specific Goals Developed at Each Practice

Every time a team meets for practice, set one to three measurable goals that the team can work on during the session. They should fit within the framework of the season's overarching goal. For example, if the season objective is to become an excellent passing team, the first practice would be set up as follows.

Practice One: Learning to Execute Short Give-and-Go Passes

Develop the following four skills required to succeed:

1. Change of direction techniques without a ball. Teach each player to drive off the inside foot in order to move quickly in a different direction. Incorporate an agility ladder in the practice to introduce different lateral footwork skills, followed by laterally running continuously over three six-inch hurdles, set three feet apart, and balancing on the inside foot with the opposite foot raised off the ground at the end of each three-hurdle run before changing direction back through the hurdles the opposite way.

2. Execution of quick, short, accurate passes. Set up eighteen cones as golf holes (place holes at different distances). A player starts by seeing how long it takes to successfully pass one ball and hit all eighteen cones. Passes that hit a cone must be at least six feet away in order to finish that hole. Start players off one at a time and time how long it takes to successfully maneuver through the entire course. Stagger-start each player

after one completes three holes, with another coach or parent timing each player. By staggering starts, you can have up to six players moving through the course at any one time.

3. Short, accurate passes followed immediately by sprinting to another spot on the field. Players learn not to hesitate after making an accurate pass. After passing, they immediately sprint to another open area on the field to receive a return pass. This can be practiced individually by setting up three twelve-inch hurdles five yards apart on a diagonal with three soccer balls per player. The player begins by taking two touches upfield, then attempts to pass the first ball along the ground with his right foot through the hurdle three yards to his left. After executing the pass, the player immediately accelerates to the second ball, placed five yards downfield, and passes that ball through the second hurdle to his left with his right foot. Then the player sprints to a third ball five yards farther downfield, passes it through the third hurdle, and concludes the drill by sprinting past a finish line marked another five yards downfield. Repeat in the other direction using the left foot. Count the number of passes that travel through each hurdle and time how long it takes to successfully finish the course. Add a three-second penalty for every ball that does not make it through a hurdle.

4. Receiving a pass and immediately passing the ball back to your teammate upfield while sprinting to receive the next pass. Set up two rows of cones ten

BEYOND WINNING—A NEW PARADIGM FOR YOUTH SPORTS COMPETITION

yards apart and ten yards across from each other. One player starts with a ball at the first cone on the left, and one player stands at the first cone downfield on the right. Player One passes the ball diagonally upfield to Player Two, then sprints upfield to the second cone in the row on his side to receive a return pass from Player Two. Passes go back and forth as players sprint from one cone to another. Passes should be accurate and should be received cleanly and passed back diagonally upfield toward the next cone as quickly as possible. Pairs can be timed to see how long it takes them to complete six consecutive give-and-go passes upfield. Adjust their scores for accuracy.

• • •

If you develop five to seven additional sessions similar to this one, you'll have created a season's worth of developmental practices all centered around improving a team's passing ability. Such sessions are much more productive than traditional youth league games. Players develop fundamental personal and team skills much faster and are able to monitor their individual improvement as well as the team's. No player stands around or sits on a bench. All players, regardless of skill level, are learning and improving.

Time to Change the Paradigm

We hope that this final chapter has provided you with a clear picture of the concrete ways that the Whole Child and Whole Youth Sports ethos can inform athletic and sports-specific training, and we hope that in exploring the dynamics between sports parents and their children, telling poignant stories, and answering parents' burning questions throughout the book we have provided some guidance and concrete solutions that can be directly applied to make your child's sporting experience more enjoyable and worthwhile. Our practical, holistic approach to the development of children and young people expands the definition of success. Yes, we incorporate winning, but our primary focus is fun, safe, developmentally appropriate training, practice, and competition.

We've reached the tipping point in youth sports. And it's up to us, as parents, to create a healthier, less toxic youth sports culture. Our children need us, and we need each other. Together we can all work to design and build a road map for change.

Acknowledgments

A simple and heartfelt acknowledgment to my two co-authors Luis Fernando and Scott who made the many days of meeting, planning, and writing in "the cabin" in upstate New York so much fun and so very inspiring. Here's to the future, gentlemen! Also, many thanks to Lara Asher, our editor who "got it" from the beginning to the end.   KJP

Scott and Kim, one could not ask for two more passionate, commited partners and champions of children's sports. A special thank you to our editor, Lara Asher, who recognized the value in our message from the get-go and shepherded it to fruition. And to every coach I've ever had, on or off the field, starting with the first: Mom. Most importantly, thank you dear Mary, Chai, Isabel, Will, Gabriel, and Inigo. You are the reasons why.   LFLL

To my two other authors and friends for the time, laughter, and deep discussions that developed into a great book and cause. I would also like to recognize all the teachers in my life who made learning fun and engaging. However this book would not be possible without some of the special times I've spent learning from and working with Bill Walsh, Pete Carroll, Mike Woicik, Jerry Horowitz, Chris DiCintio, and hundreds of youth and high school coaches.   SL

Bibliography

Biddulph, Steve. *Raising Boys: Why Boys Are Different—and How to Help Them Become Happy and Well-Balanced Men.* Berkeley, CA: Celestial Arts, 1998.

Bigelow, Bob, Tom Moroney, and Linda Hall. *Just Let the Kids Play: How to Stop Other Adults from Ruining Your Child's Fun and Success in Youth Sports.* Deerfield Beach, FL: Health Communications, 2001.

Cantu, Robert, and Mark Hyman. *Concussions and Our Kids: America's Leading Expert on How to Protect Young Athletes and Keep Sports Safe.* New York: Houghton Mifflin Harcourt, 2012.

de Lench, Brooke. *Home Team Advantage: The Critical Role of Mothers in Youth Sports.* New York: Harper Collins, 2006.

Dweck, Carol. *Mindset: The New Psychology of Success.* New York: Ballantine Books, 2006.

Elkind, David. *The Hurried Child.* 25th Anniversary Edition. New York: Da Capo, 2006.

Engh, Fred. *Why Johnny Hates Sports: Why Organized Sports Are Failing Our Children and What We Can Do About It.* Garden City Park, NY: Square One Publishers, 2002.

Farrey, Tom. *Game On: How the Pressure to Win at All Costs Endangers Youth Sports and What Parents Can Do About It.* New York: ESPN Books, 2008.

Fish, Joel, with Susan Magee. *101 Ways to Be a Terrific Sports Parent.* New York: Simon & Schuster, 2003.

Ginsburg, Richard D., and Stephen Durant, with Amy Baltzell. *Whose Game Is It, Anyway?: A Guide to Helping Your Child Get the Most from Sports, Organized by Age and Stage.* New York: Houghton Mifflin Harcourt, 2006.

Goleman, Daniel. *Emotional Intelligence: Why It Can Matter More than IQ.* New York: Bantam, 1995.

Hyman, Mark. *The Most Expensive Game in Town: The Rising Cost of Youth Sports and the Toll on Today's Families.* Boston: Beacon Press, 2012.

———. *Until It Hurts: America's Obsession with Youth Sports and How It Harms Our Kids.* Boston: Beacon Press, 2009.

Lancaster, Scott B. *Fair Play: Making Organized Sports a Great Experience for Your Kids.* New York: Prentice Hall, 2002.

Lancaster, Scott B., and Radu Teodorescu. *Athletic Fitness for Kids.* Champaign, IL: Human Kinetics, 2008.

Lanza, Mike. *Playborhood: Turn Your Neighborhood into a Place for Play.* Menlo Park, CA: Free Play Press, 2012.

Payne, Kim John, and Kate Hammond. *Games Children Play: How Games and Sport Help Children Develop.* Gloucestershire, UK: Hawthorne, 1997.

Payne, Kim John, with Lisa M. Ross. *Simplicity Parenting: Using the Extraordinary Power of Less to Raise Calmer, Happier and More Secure Kids.* New York: Ballantine Books, 2009.

Siegel, Daniel. *The Developing Mind.* New York: Guilford, 1999.

Siegel, Daniel, and Mary Hartzell. *Parenting from the Inside Out: How a Deeper Self-Understanding Can Help You Raise Children Who Thrive.* New York: Jeremy, Tarcher, 2003.

Siegel, Daniel, and Tina Payne Bryson. *The Whole-Brain Child: 12 Revolutionary Strategies to Nurture Your Child's Developing Mind.* New York: Bantam Books, 2012.

Thompson, Michael, and Catherine O'Neill Grace, with Lawrence J. Cohen. *Best Friends, Worst Enemies: Understanding the Social Lives of Children.* New York: Ballantine Books, 2001.

Index

action sports, 170–72

adaptability, 71–73, 76–77

aggressiveness, 164, 167

agility ladders, 135

agility training, 135, 174

Air Raider (game), 205–6

anger triggers, 25–28

ankle jumps, 198

assertiveness, 164, 165–67

athletic movement training, 167–70

athletic potential, fostering, 134–38

athletic skill development, 199–200

Back Space (game), 205

backyard golf, 131–32

balance, physical, 135, 144–45, 174, 175, 180–83, 184–85

balanced youth sports experience, 183–88

Balance in Motion (game), 144–45

baseball, 56–59, 203–4

basketball, 204–5

Berry, Raymond, 186

Biddulph, Steve, 97

Blind Prisoner (game), 205–6

boredom, 90–93

break from sports, taking, 19–21

Brommer, Alice, 19–21

Brommer, Lisa, 19–21

Brommer, Thomas, 19, 20–21

bullying, 102–3, 105–7

Cantu, Robert, 33

cardiovascular training, 174

Christakis, Erika, 78, 80

Christakis, Nicholas, 78, 80

coaches. *See also specific topics*
    bullying culture, role in, 105–7
    choosing, 148
    education and training, 196
    ego driven, 145–47
    favoritism, 122–23
    parents as first, 126–32
    women, 138–42

cognitive development, 188

community service projects, 118–19

concussions, 33

core (hip and trunk muscle groups), 181

creativity, 71–73, 80–84

criticism, 23–25

Crossing the Line strategy, 112–13

dehumanization, 102–3, 109

de Lench, Brooke, 139–40

developmental stages, 11–14, 73–74, 93. *See also specific stages*

Dicari, Fran, 157–59

Disapprove, Affirm, Redirect strategy, 98

Disapprove–Affirm–Discover–Do Over (DADD) strategy, 114–16

Dweck, Carol, 73, 77

dynamic balance and multiterrain stations, 137–38

easygoing/phlegmatic temperament, 115
entitlement, sense of, 118–19
equipment for home coaching, 135–36
executive function, 78–79
expectations, 19–21, 61–64, 159, 161
experiential learning, 143–45

faking injuries, 68–69
family time, erosion of, 162–64
Farrey, Tom, 51, 153, 154
favoritism, 122–23
financial costs of youth sports, 151, 157–61
flag football, 191–95
flighty/sanguine temperament, 116
football, 191–95, 200–201, 202–3
forward walking lunges, 199
Franklin, Benjamin, 143
Fraone, Jennifer Sabatini, 92
friendships, 54–56
Frisbee golf, 131
Frisbees, 131, 136, 204–5
Frobel, Friedrich, 93

game, responding to, 41–42
gender differences in play, 96–98
genocide, 102
goals, 65–66
golden sports moments, 28–30
golf, 130–32
Gualtiere, John, 191–92, 193, 194–95
gymnastics mats, 136

hand walk, 198

Harding, John, 149, 151, 152
Healy, Aiden, 193, 194
Healy, Owen, 193–94
Healy, Rob, 193–94
history of specific sports, 185
Home Run Derby (game), 203–4
Hyman, Mark, 33
hypercompetitiveness, 100–102

imagination, 80–84
individual versus team sports, 132–33
injuries, 31, 32–33, 58, 68–69, 176–79
introverted children, 132–33, 165

jerseys, wearing to school, 118–19
jumping jacks, 198

Lanza, Mike, 74, 79
learning, experiential, 143–45
Levy, Jenny, 71–72, 74, 81, 91–92, 172
local investments, 161
losing, moving on after, 40–41
lunges, 199

MacAskill, Danny, 171
media consumption, limiting, 120–21
moms as coaches, 138–42

narratives, alternative, 41–42
National Football League's Junior Player Development program, 200–201
national tournaments/championships, 149, 151–53

NERF balls, 136

obstacle courses, 134–35, 136–38, 183
off-season, 163, 179–80, 209
Oksanen, Jussi, 160, 172
organized sports, age for starting, 47–50
Ossining Little League Football, 192–95
overprotectiveness, 30–33
overreacting, 26
overtraining, 19–21

Packer, Steven, 194
pain, playing through, 30–33
paradigm, new, 195–96
parents. *See also specific topics*
   as child's first coach, 126–32
   expectations, 19–21, 61–64
   putting down others, 107–9
   sports biographies, 22, 24, 28–30, 34–36
   triggers, anger, 25–28
Parker, Kevin K., 73
passes, short give-and-go, 211–13
pendulum of sports experience, 155–56
pitchbacks, 135
pitching, 56–59
play
   benefits, 75–76, 87–89, 94
   development and, 11–14, 73–74, 93
   gender differences, 96–98
   importance of, 79–80
   lack of, 74–75, 94
   manifesto, 79

   in practice sessions, 201–6
   stages, 47–48, 84–85, 88–89
   team benefits, 84–87
Playborhood Manifesto, 79
popularity, attempts to gain, 110–11
positions, team, 56–59, 122–25, 200–201
postpubescence, 174, 175. *See also* Stage Four
power training, 174, 175
practice, dislike of, 64–66
prepubescence, 174, 175. *See also* Stage One; Stage Two
pressure, 19–21, 43–46, 60–61
Preview and Review strategy, 113–14
proprioception, 174, 175, 180
puberty, 174, 175. *See also* Stage Two; Stage Three; Stage Four
put-downs, 107–16

quitting sports, 64–65, 67–68

Receiving/Defending (game), 143–44
Red Zone (game), 202–3
reframing, 108
Roth, Neil A., 56–57, 58, 68–69, 74
rules, sports, 185–86

scoring alternatives, 209
self-coaching skills, 196
self-correcting, 108–9
sensitive/melancholic temperament, 115
simplifying, 163

skateboarding, 170–72
skill competitions, self-measuring, 206–8
snag golf, 132
soccer, 169, 209
speed, 168
sports biographies, parents', 22, 24, 28–30, 34–36
sports equipment for home coaching, 135–36
sports violence on television, 119–21
squats, 198
Stage One, 12, 128–29, 174, 175
Stage Two, 12–13, 128–29, 174, 175
Stage Three, 13, 129, 174, 175
Stage Four, 13–14, 174, 175
Steiner, Rudolf, 93
Step2 balance balls, 136
strength training, 174
stress, 19–21, 43–46, 60–61
stretching, 174, 175
strong/choleric temperament, 115

Target Ball (game), 205
team captains, 116–18
team competition, progression toward, 208–9
team *versus* individual sports, 132–33
television, sports violence on, 119–21
temperaments, 115–16, 132, 165
tennis balls, 136
theme, overarching, 211–13

Thompson, Michael, 110
training and conditioning activities, 173–75
training session blueprint, 196–213
athletic skill development, 199–200
play and games, 201–6
position, training for every, 200–201
skill competitions, self-measuring, 206–8
team competition, progression toward, 208–9
theme, overarching, 211–13
warm-up, 197–99
trash talk, 107–16
travel teams, 50–53
triggers, anger, 25–28
twenty-yard lateral lunges, 199

Ultimate Football (game), 202

vestibular system, 180
Vew-Do NUB Boards, 135, 182
vision, 180
volleyball, 205–6

Wagner, Noel, 77
warming up, 56–57, 59, 197–99
winning, overemphasis on, 3, 36–39
women coaches, 138–42
Wooden, John, 37

Zitoli, Andrew, 105–7

About the Authors

Luis Fernando Llosa is a writer, editor, speaker, and investigative reporter. He joined *Sports Illustrated* as a general reporter in 1998, after working at *Fortune* and *Money* magazines. His first investigation, in 2001, exposed Little Leaguer Danny Almonte's age fraud, ranked among the top ten sports scandals of the past century. In 2004 he reported from Mexico and the Dominican Republic for "Totally Juiced," *Sports Illustrated*'s National Magazine Award finalist in the reporting category.

In 2006 Llosa co-wrote "The Mexican Connection," which exposed the largest steroid pipeline in history and detailed the DEA probe of the illegal importation of 80 percent of the steroids into the U.S. Over the next four years he reported on the pervasive steroid use in sports, exposing athletes who received steroids and/or HGH, among them MLB stars Gary Matthews, Jr., David Bell, and Troy Glaus, boxer Evander Holyfield, and two 2008 Jamaican Olympic track stars. Llosa, who also broke stories on boxer Shane Mosley's use of EPO and testosterone and the federal indictment of New York Mets clubhouse employee Kirk Rodomski, was the most sourced journalist in the Mitchell Report on Steroids in Major League Baseball.

Youth sports has been Llosa's primary passion, both privately and professionally. He has coached soccer for twenty years and, in 2008, co-wrote "Sins of a Father" an SI exclusive about a 13-year-old in-line skater injected with HGH and testosterone by his father, who became the first parent ever convicted and jailed for providing his child with steroids.

Llosa has made more than 100 national and local television and radio appearances, including on CBS Evening News,

CNN, CNN en Español, FOX News, FOX & Friends, Greta Van Susteren, Nancy Grace, Univision, NPR, and ESPN Radio to discuss steroid investigations and other sports-related issues.

Scott Lancaster has over twenty-five years of experience developing athletic and fitness programs for the National Football League, PGA of America, Arena Football, United Soccer, and Fairmont Hotels & Resorts. He has also developed fitness/sports products for Step2, one of the nation's leading toy manufacturers. He has created comprehensive (individual and team) athletic sports curricula and implemented and managed those programs at both local and national levels.

Lancaster is the author of two youth athletic and fitness books: *Fair Play: Making Organized Sports a Great Experience for Your Kids* (Prentice House, 2002), and *Athletic Fitness for Kids* (Human Kinetics, 2008), and hosted a national sports talk radio show on SiriusXM that focused on youth and high school sports.

Kim John Payne, M.Ed., has been a school counselor, adult educator, consultant, researcher, educator, and private family counselor for over thirty years. He regularly gives keynote addresses at international conferences for educators, parents, and therapists and runs workshops around the world. In each role, he has helped children, adolescents, and families explore issues such as social difficulties with siblings and classmates, attention and behavioral issues at home and school, and emotional issues such as defiance, aggression, addiction, and low self-esteem as well as the vital role that living a balanced simple life plays.

He is founding director of the Simplicity Project and the Center for Social Sustainability and the author of *Simplicity*

Parenting: Using the Extraordinary Power of Less to Raise Calmer, Happier and More Secure Kids (Ballantine Books/Random House, 2009). He also wrote *Games Children Play* (Hawthorn Press, 1996) and is currently writing *The Soul of Discipline* (Ballantine Books/Random House, 2014). Payne has appeared frequently on television (including ABC, NBC, CBS, and Fox), on radio with the BBC, Sirius/XM, CBC & NPR, and has been featured in *Time* magazine, the *Chicago Tribune, Parenting, Mothering,* and the *Los Angeles Times.* He is a writer for *The Huffington Post.*

Payne strives to deepen understanding and give practical tools for life that arise out of the burning social issues of our time. He is based in Northampton, Massachusetts, with his wife and two children. www.simplicityparenting.com